Computer & Internet Dictionary

Lisa A. Bucki

Acknowledgements

Chris Katsaropoulos of DDC asked me to write this book, and I thank him for renewing our acquaintance in such a great way. Kudos to Jennifer Frew for leading this book through the production process and Howard Peterson for ensuring its accuracy. I would also like to thank others at DDC who had a hand in the process, including Peter McCarthy and the production, marketing, and sales teams. Finally, I appreciate the support of my husband, Steve, and my dog, Bo, who help me keep the words flowing.   *Lisa A. Bucki*

Managing Editor
Jennifer Frew

Technical Editor
Howard Peterson

Layout
Elsa Johannesson
Elviro Padro
Paul Wray

Acquisitions Manager
Chris Katsaropoulos

English Editors
Emily Hay
Monique Peterson

Design
Elsa Johannesson

Cover Design
Amy Capuano

Copyright© 1999 by DDC Publishing, Inc.
Published by DDC Publishing, Inc.
The information contained herein is copyrighted by DDC Publishing, Inc.
All right reserved, including the right to reproduce this book or portions thereof in any form whatsoever. For information, address DDC Publishing, Inc., 275 Madison Avenue, 12th Floor, New York, New York 10016
Internet address: *http://www.ddcpub.com*

Cat. No.:   G42
ISBN: 1-56243-700-3
First DDC Publishing, Inc. Printing:
10   9   8   7   6   5   4   3   2   1
Printed in the United States of America.

Microsoft®, Internet Explorer, MS-DOS®, Word 97®, and Windows 95 are registered trademarks of Microsoft Corporation.
Corel and WordPerfect are registered trademarks of Corel Corporations or Corel Corporations Limited.
Netscape™, Netscape™ Communications logo, Netscape™ Communications Corporation, Netscape™ Communications, Netscape Mail™, and Netscape™ Navigator are all trademarks of Netscape™ Communications Corporation.
Microsoft® and Windows® are registered trademarks of the Microsoft Corporation.
Yahoo!™ and Yahoo™ logo are trademarks of Yahoo!™
LYCOS™, LYCOS™ logo are trademarks of LYCOS™.
AltaVista™ and the AltaVista™ logo are trademarks of AltaVista Technology, Inc.

Introduction

If you need to know more about computers, the Internet, and new technology in general, this book is for you.

This dictionary zeros in on 1,001 of the most important terms you need to understand, work with, talk about, and even buy computers and software, including terms about the Internet and World Wide Web.

Like other dictionaries, this one presents terms in A to Z order. Along the way, you'll find special elements that highlight key information:

 This icon appears beside the name of any term that deals with communications, including networking, connecting computers via a modem, or connecting to the Internet. You'll find nearly 200 of these.

 Tip boxes like these highlight extra tidbits of information, or ideas and steps to save you time.

This book presents command choices by giving the menu name, followed by subsequent command names, all of them separated using the | (pipe) character. So, Insert|Picture|Clip Art means to click the Insert menu, click the Picture command, and then click the Clip Art command in the submenu that appears.

Keep this book handy, and you'll soon feel confident and comfortable every time you work with computers.

Best of luck,

Lisa A. Bucki

Characters #s

* You can use the asterisk symbol (*) primarily in two ways while computing. The asterisk can function as a wildcard character, representing multiple characters when you're searching for a file or performing other file-related operations. For example, you could enter **ail* to match files named *trail*, *mail*, or *retail*. Or, you can use the asterisk in an e-mail message to emphasize a word as if you had italicized it, as in: Please be *careful* when you drive. (See also *wildcard*.)

 You can use the Start | Find | Files or Folders command to search for a file in Windows 95 or 98.

. (pronounced star dot star) This group of wildcard characters can represent all the characters in a file name, or the ending characters and the file name extension when you're searching for a file. Entering *.* on its own finds all the files on a disk or in a folder. Entering *m*.** matches all files starting with M, including *memo.doc*, *mortgage.doc*, or *mortgage.exe*. (See also *extension*.)

**** The backslash character separates the disk, folder(s), and file name in the path name for a file, as in *C:\Program Files\Microsoft Office\Office\Excel.exe*. (See also *path*.)

/ The forward slash character separates the parts of the URL address for a Web page, as in *http://www.ddcpub.com*. (See also *URL*.)

? The question mark serves as a wildcard character, representing a single character when you search for a file. For instance, entering *chap??.doc* matches files including *chap01.doc*, *chap23.doc*, or *chapaa.doc*.

1-2-3 (see Lotus 1-2-3)

3.5-inch disk A floppy disk that has its magnetic storage media encased within a 3 ½-inch square rigid plastic case (see Figure 0.1). You can copy your computer files onto a floppy disk to create a spare copy of the files or to move files from one computer to another. Most floppy disks in use today feature high density (HD) capacity, meaning they can hold up to 1.44M of information. (See also *LS-120 disk*.)

1

Figure 0.1 3 ½-inch floppy disks

3D (or 3-D) 3D carries a few different meanings in computing today. It can refer to a computer's ability to display graphics that appear three-dimensional or play sound that seems to come from multiple sources (called "Surround Sound," in some cases). 3D also can describe a drawing, painting, or animation. You can also create 3D ranges in some spreadsheet programs; these ranges span not only a block of cells but also multiple worksheets in the current file.

10/100 BaseT This term identifies Ethernet networking components (for a Local Area Network) that support two types of Ethernet: Fast Ethernet, which can transfer data at up to 100 Mbps; and regular Ethernet, which works at 10 Mbps. Mbps stands for megabits per second, or 1,000,000 bits per second. (See also *bit*.)

440BX (100 MHz chipset) This set of chips on a computer's motherboard enables the system's bus to transfer data between the computer's internal components at up to 100 MHz. Faster internal components can operate more quickly under faster bus speeds. (See also *bus, MHz*.)

486 (also 80486, pronounced 80-486) The dominant family of CPUs offered in PCs from approximately 1989 to 1993. 486 CPUs use a 32-bit structure, enabling them to access more main memory and operate significantly faster than earlier CPUs. While 486 processors no longer appear in new systems, you may encounter older systems using this CPU. (See also *central processing unit*.)

A

Abort To stop a program or command before it finishes, often by pressing [Esc], [Ctrl]+[C], or the Break key on the keyboard. Sometimes, when an operation "hangs," or stalls your computer, it presents a dialog box offering a button you can click to abort the operation.

About dialog box A dialog box you can display to find out what version of a program you're using and to view the registered serial number for your copy of the program (see Figure A.1). You typically display the About dialog box by choosing the About (*program name*) command from the Help menu in the program.

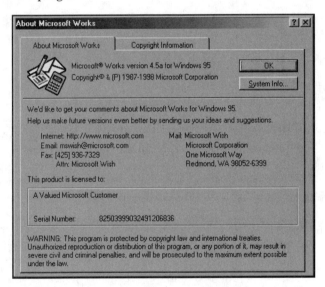

Figure A.1 Find out about your version of a program in the About dialog box.

absolute reference In a spreadsheet program, an absolute reference in a formula always refers to the same cell, even if you copy the formula to another location. For example, if a formula performs a calculation that multiplies a percentage value in one cell, such as B3, by values in other cells, you always want the formula to refer to cell B3. Spreadsheet programs usually require you to insert dollar signs, as in *B3*, to create an absolute reference to a cell address. (See also *address*.)

accelerator board A circuit board that you install in a computer to replace the CPU with faster circuitry. You'll likely encounter only accelerator boards if you're dealing with a system that uses a 486 or older CPU.

Access (Microsoft Access) This database program, published by Microsoft, enables you to store lists of information, such as a list of customer names and addresses or a list of all the audio CDs you've bought. The Microsoft Office Professional Edition suite of software includes Microsoft Access. (See also *database program*.)

access time Access time covers two areas: how fast a computer's memory (RAM) can move information into the CPU; and how fast a hard disk, floppy disk, removable disk, or CD-ROM drive can read information. You'll find memory access time measured in ns (nanoseconds). You may find disk (drive) access time expressed in ms (milliseconds), but you may also find disk speed expressed in terms of the data transfer rate, the speed at which the drive transfers information. Data transfer is typically measured in MB/s (megabytes per second).

> If you're buying or upgrading a computer, remember that *smaller* measurements for memory access time or disk access time are better—indicating faster memory or a faster drive. Conversely, *larger* data transfer measurements indicate a faster drive.

accounting software Software you use to perform accounting functions. Business accounting software like Peachtree or QuickBooks typically enables you to track assets, expenses, inventory, and payroll, as well as providing invoicing and reporting features. You can use personal accounting software such as Quicken or Microsoft Money to record transactions for your bank accounts, print checks, monitor credit card balances and investment returns, and review reports such as net worth reports.

active Active indicates that a program window, file window, dialog box, or area within a program holds the insertion point. Any action you perform or command you select occurs in the active program window, file window, dialog box, or other program area. (See also *active window, current cell or selection,* and *current file.*)

Active Desktop This new feature of Windows 98 and/or Microsoft Internet Explorer 4 enables you to set up the Windows desktop to display information downloaded from the Internet, such as news headlines and stock prices. You also can set up the Active Desktop to download updates automatically.

active matrix A type of display for notebook computers that offers better resolution and contrast than do the older passive matrix displays. Active matrix displays also work more quickly because a separate transistor

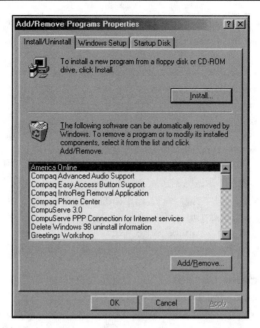

Figure A.2 Remove a program installed under Windows using this dialog box.

address An address tells a program where to find particular information. Each type of address uses its own syntax—rules identifying how many characters make up the address, what type of characters can be used, etc. The computer itself also uses addresses to identify areas in the Random Access Memory (RAM) so the CPU can retrieve information from the right location as needed. (See also *cell address, e-mail address, memory*, and *IP Address*.)

Address Book Most e-mail programs, whether used for an internal network or for Internet communication, offer an Address Book into which you can enter the name and e-mail address for each person with whom you correspond. Some Address Books enable you to capture additional information such as home and business phone numbers, mailing addresses, and fax numbers.

ADSL (asymmetric digital subscriber line) One of the emerging technologies for enabling analog phone lines to carry digital signals for faster Internet access. With ADSL services, users are able to receive information at 1.5-7 Mbps and send information at 64-640 Kbps. To implement ADSL service, phone companies need to install special hardware, and users need to install special modems. (See also *bps*.)

controls each screen pixel (small dot of colored light). Most notebook computers sold today use active matrix technology.

active window The file window that holds the insertion point (for a word processor or presentation graphics program) or cell selector (in a spreadsheet or database program). Anything you type appears in the active window document, page, spreadsheet, or database table. Any command you select also applies to the active window.

ActiveX A method developed to animate information on Web pages. In particular, Web-page developers often use ActiveX components to retrieve specific information from a database or a text file. Your Web browser must have ActiveX support capability to work well with ActiveX. The most recent versions of the top browsers do support ActiveX.

adapter (also called card) A separate circuit board that plugs into a slot on the computer's motherboard to add new features or upgrade existing features. For example, a video adapter card can enable your computer's monitor to work more quickly. An SCSI adapter card can enable you to attach fast SCSI add-ons, like a SCSI hard disk, to your computer. Your modem also might be an adapter card. Adapter cards give you a lot of flexibility in determining what features you want your system to offer. (See also *motherboard* and *SCSI*.)

> If an advertisement for a computer says that it has a feature, like video capability, on board, that typically means the capability has been built into the motherboard. On-board features don't prevent you from adding an adapter card to upgrade that feature in the future.

add-in program An add-in program adds features to an application. For example, you can load the Solver add-in to Excel and use it to find the best answer to a complex problem with multiple variables.

Add/Remove Programs A feature in Windows 95 and 98 that enables you to install and remove programs more easily. Before Windows 95, you often had to delete a program manually from a computer's hard disk. Then, references to the deleted program could remain in key system files and affect the computer's performance. When you use the Add/Remove Programs Properties dialog box (see Figure A.2) to delete a program, Windows deletes all the program files and cleans the vast majority of references to the program from Windows system files.

> To display the Add/Remove Programs Properties dialog box, choose Start | Settings | Control Panel, and then double-click the Add/Remove Programs button.

AGP graphics AGP stands for Accelerated Graphics Port. Intel introduced the AGP bus in 1997 to carry display (video) information separately within the computer. This enables the computer to display demanding, memory-intensive, 3D graphics much more quickly. The AGP bus most benefits displays for 3D games and animations. AGP graphics cards plug into a special slot on the motherboard. (See also *bus*.)

 If you're a heavy game user, look for AGP graphics (video) capabilities when you're shopping for a new computer.

AIFF One of the Apple QuickTime audio (sound) file formats. Although Apple's file formats were developed to be used primarily on Macintosh computers, you may find AIFF files on Web pages that you can download and play on your Windows-based computer.

alias (also called shortcut) An alias, or shortcut, serves as a link to a file in another location. For example, you can create a shortcut in one Windows folder to open a file stored in another folder. The alias, or shortcut, can use a completely different name than the original file it represents. Aliases make it easy for you to create several locations from which you can access or open a file.

alignment Refers to how information lines up relative to the document margins or the boundaries of a cell or text box in a document. Figure A.3 illustrates various alignments.

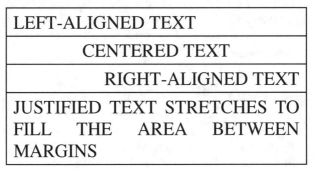

Figure A.3 *Most applications enable you to align text in various ways.*

all caps Refers to displaying words in all capital letters. Figure A.3 also illustrates this text formatting method. You can type text in all caps by pressing the Caps Lock key. Press the Caps Lock key again to resume typing in upper- and lowercase. (See also *small caps*.)

 Some programs, such as Microsoft Word, also enable you to convert text to all caps after typing it. For example, you can select the text in Word and press Shift+F3 to move between lowercase, initial caps, and all caps.

alphanumeric characters Labels, words, or phrases that include both letters and numbers, as in *A139X*.

alphanumeric sort A sorting method that considers both letters and numbers in a label, word, or phrase. For example, an alphanumeric sort might sort items beginning with punctuation marks or symbols first (!,$, %, or &, for example), then items beginning with numbers. Items beginning with letters are sorted last.

Alt key A key you press in conjunction with another keyboard key to select a command or run a macro. For example, in most applications you can press [Alt]+[F] to open the File menu. You can also press [Alt] in conjunction with one of the Function keys at the top of the keyboard to perform a command or action. (See also *Function keys*.)

AMD (Advanced Micro Devices) A company that produces CPUs that are comparable to and compete with CPUs from the industry leader, Intel. A new PC with an AMD CPU might cost $300 less than a PC with a comparable Intel CPU. The AMD-K6 MMX/266 CPU, for example, offers roughly comparable speed and features as an Intel Pentium II/266 CPU. (See also *central processing unit*, *Cyrix*, *Intel*, and *MMX*.)

America Online (AOL) The world's leading online service, with 10 million or more users who log on to share information and e-mail, or connect with the Internet. Figure A.4 shows the most recent version of AOL's software, which you use to access the service. The Figure also illustrates AOL's channels, or topic areas. (See also *online community*.)

Figure A.4 Log on to AOL with AOL software.

analog Representing or transmitting information in a continuous, wave-like form that varies depending on the changing values or amplitude. For example, a turntable reads wavy, analog grooves from an LP's surface and amplifies the resulting sound. In contrast, digital information uses discrete values, recorded at a particular point in time or in a particular location. For example, CD player reads reflective, specific spots that represent digital values on the CD's surface, converts the digital information to sound, and amplifies the sound.

animation A moving computer image that combines multiple objects that change in position. You may have seen animated banners and graphics on Web pages, or you may have seen special animated mouse pointers in programs. Numerous programs enable you to create various types of animations and animated objects.

> Animated graphics consume considerable system and video RAM. If your system bombs out when you try to run an animation or if the animation runs in a jerky fashion, you may need to upgrade your system's RAM or video RAM.

anonymous log-in Certain types of sites on the Internet require that you log on, or provide a name and password, to view the site's information. With many FTP sites, you also can use anonymous log-in, which gives you access to certain public areas on the site. You choose the anonymous log-in method in your FTP software, such as CuteFTP, a shareware program. (See also *FTP*.)

answer mode Communications software can be specified to answer incoming calls automatically with your modem. Generally, the communications software program must be open for the modem to answer the call.

antialiasing A feature in some software programs that softens the jaggies (stairstep effect) that occur when you select a large letter size or make an object with an outline very large. On the downside, antialiasing can give a somewhat fuzzy appearance to letters and outlines.

antivirus This term applies to any software or software feature that scans your system and files for viruses. Most antivirus programs also can clean or remove the virus from the affected system areas or files. Typically, you can choose to scan for viruses either automatically or manually. (See also *virus*.)

API (Application Programming Interface) The specific set of programming rules, methods, statements, and other technical tools a programmer uses to create a program that runs under a particular operating system. For example, to create Windows programs, programmers follow the Windows API. The API helps applications look consistent and work consistently with the operating system. (See also *operating system* and *Visual Basic*.)

append To add information to the end of an existing file or database table.

Apple Computer, Inc. The company that manufactures Power Macintosh desktop PCs and PowerBook notebook PCs. Apple's most recent models use the G3 CPU. Newer Apple systems run the Mac OS 8 operating system. Because Apple's systems use a different CPU and operating system, file and disk formats aren't generally compatible with Windows-based machines.

 To read a floppy or removable disk from a Windows-based system on a Mac system, use a program called Apple File Exchange or an OS 8 feature called PC Exchange. To read a floppy or removable disk from a Mac system using a Windows-based system, you can buy and install the MacOpener program.

applet A small program performing a specific function, such as the CD Player applet in Windows or the Microsoft Org chart applet in Office applications. You can access Windows applets by choosing Start|Programs|Accessories, and then choosing the applet to start. Choose a command or button to start the applet.

application (see program)

Computer & Internet Dictionary

application window The window that opens on the Windows desktop when you start an application. The application window holds a separate window for each file you open and create in the application.

Approach The database program published by Lotus Development Corporation. Lotus sells Approach separately or as part of the SmartSuite software suite. Approach provides relational database capabilities. (See also *database program*.)

archive Traditionally, this term refers to a specialized backup file created by a backup program. More commonly, however, the term also refers to a special type of file that holds multiple compressed files. (See also *compressed file*.)

argument A value or text string you include in a programming statement or in a command within a program; the statement or command uses the argument information when it runs. You also use arguments in spreadsheet formulas that include functions. For example, the argument(s) you specify for the SUM function tells the spreadsheet program what values to add or which cells hold those values. Figure A.5 shows an example of a formula with a function and its arguments. (See also *formula* and *function*.)

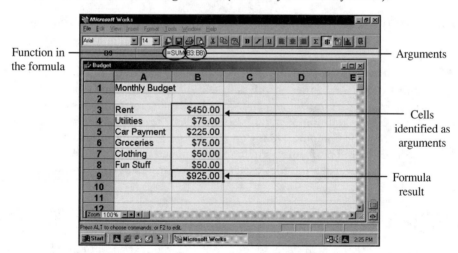

Figure A.5 The arguments B3:B8 tell the SUM function in the formula to add the values in cells B3 through B8.

arrow key Literally, the keyboard keys that have arrows on them. Most keyboards offer up, down, left, and right arrow keys, but some also include diagonal arrow keys. Usually, you press an arrow key to move the insertion point in a document file. Pressing the up arrow or down arrow moves the insertion point up or down one row. Pressing the left arrow or right arrow moves the insertion point one character to the left or right. (See also *insertion point*.)

arrow pointer The mouse pointer you see on the screen changes shape depending on what you're doing or to what you are pointing in the program. An arrow pointer generally means you can click to select the button, command, or text appearing under the pointer. The arrow pointer may change colors, but it most often appears in white with a black outline. (See also *I-beam pointer*.)

ascender An ascender appears on certain lower-case letters, such as b, d, f, h, k, and t. The ascender consists of any part of the letter that stretches above the main body of the letter. For example, the vertical line that stretches above the loop in a b or d is the ascender for those letters. Ascenders help make lowercase letters easier to read by providing greater variation in letter shapes. (See also *descender*.)

ascending order Ascending order refers to text information alphabetized in A to Z order or numbers ordered from the smallest value to the largest.

ASCII (pronounced as-key) ASCII stands for American Standard Code for Information Interchange. It refers to a standard set of characters that virtually all programs understand. The ASCII character set consists of mostly letters and numbers, but also includes a few symbols and codes for controlling the computer. Many applications enable you to save your files in ASCII or plain text format, which exclude special formatting and characters, but make the files easier for other programs to open.

ASCII art Years ago, some computer users began combining different ASCII characters in different positions to create pictures (see Figure A.6). Because earlier e-mail systems could only handle text and not graphics, users began inserting ASCII art in e-mail messages or as an part of an e-mail signature. (See also *signature* and *smiley*.)

```
        @@@@@@@@
    @@@@@@@@@@@@@@@@
  @@@@      @@@       @@@@
 @@@@       @@@        @@@@
@@@@        @@@         @@@@
@@@@        @@@         @@@@
@@@@        @@@         @@@@
@@@         @@@          @@@
@@@       @@@@@@@        @@@
@@@      @@@ @@@ @@@     @@@
@@@    @@@  @@@  @@@    @@@
@@@   @@@   @@@   @@@   @@@
@@@ @@@     @@@    @@@ @@@
@@@ @@@     @@@    @@@ @@@
@@@@@       @@@      @@@@@
 @@@@@      @@@      @@@@@
   @@@@@@@@@@@@@@@@@@@@
      @@@@@@@@@@@@@
```

Figure A.6 ASCII art uses plain text characters to create pictures.

 You can find ASCII art examples in various locations online. Try the alt.ascii-art and rec.arts.ascii Internet newsgroups for ideas about what type of ASCII art you can create.

aspect ratio This ratio compares the width of an object (such as a graphic file or chart in a document) to its height. In its original aspect ratio, the graphic looks proportional. If you don't keep the aspect ratio constant when you resize the object, you may distort the contents in the object, making it too tall and skinny or wide and flattened. Some programs will allow you to specify a constant aspect ratio for an object. Or, if you're dragging the corner of an object to resize the object, you can press and hold the Shift key while dragging to maintain the aspect ratio. (See also *graphics* and *object*.)

associate (also file association) Windows associates each file type (as identified by the three-character file name extension) with the application originally used to create that file. When you look for a file in a My Computer window, the Windows Explorer, or any Open dialog box, Windows can include an icon identifying the associated file type along with each file name. If you double-click the icon for a file in a My Computer window or in the Windows Explorer, Windows checks the file association, opens the application used to create the file, and then opens the file itself in that application. (See also *file name extension*.)

asynchronous In the computer world, this refers to transferring data in a way that's not timed or synchronized, often over traditional telephone lines. The bits flow one after another; a start bit marks the start of each bit and a stop bit marks the end of each bit for the receiving modem. When data travels asynchronously, you may see pauses in the transfer if, for example, the data flows faster than the receiving modem can receive it. (See also *bit*.)

AT bus Also called the ISA bus, this older type of system bus transfers 16 bits of data at a time. Newer buses can handle 32 or 64 bits of data at a time. So, if you're considering buying and upgrading an older system, make sure it does not use an AT bus, but instead has a 32-bit or 64-bit bus. Then, the system itself should be able to transfer data as quickly as any new component or adapter you install. (See also *bit* and *bus*.)

AT command set There's no relationship between the AT command set and the AT bus. One of the earliest modem manufactures, Hayes Microcomputer Products, developed the AT command set to control modems. Other programs can use AT commands to test the modem, tell it to dial a number, and so on. The letters AT, short for attention, start most AT commands. For example, a program might send the command ATH0 to the modem to tell the modem to hang up (disconnect).

ATA hard disk The ATA acronym identifies an "AT Attachment" interface, also called an IDE interface. ATA (IDE) hard disk drives connect to the motherboard via a 40-pin connector. The most recent type of ATA, called ATA-2 or Enhanced IDE (EIDE), enabled disk manufacturers to create more powerful hard disks. (See also *EIDE* and *IDE*.)

ATAPI (ATA Packet Interface) ATAPI enables devices that are not hard disks (like CD-ROM drives) to connect to an available ATA (IDE) connector. Such devices need ATAPI to communicate with computers because they work much differently from hard disks.

attribute Windows records key attributes about any file you save, such as its name, how large the file is, the date you created it, whether you've set the file to be read-only (so others can't change it, etc.). In Windows 95 or 98, you can right-click a file icon in a My Computer or Windows Explorer window, then click the Properties command in the shortcut menu that appears to see the properties or attributes of a file (Figure A.7). Within an application, the term attribute describes formatting you apply to text or some other object. For example, you can apply the bold attribute to selected text.

Computer & Internet Dictionary

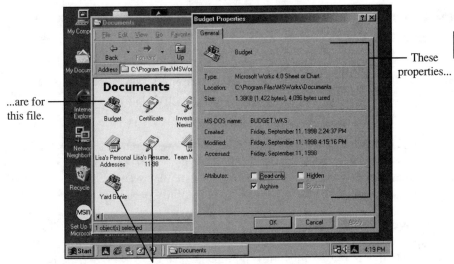

Figure A.7 You can display a file's Properties dialog box to learn details about the file.

audio Sound produced by your computer or another device.

audio CD An audio CD holds audio data in a format developed for playback via a boom box or your home stereo. Computers also can play audio CDs using audio or CD player software. (See also *CD-ROM*.)

 Your computer may come with special CD player software provided by the manufacturer of the systems sound card (the adapter that can record and play sound on your system speakers). If you don't find any such special software, choose Start | Programs | Accessories | Entertainment | CD Player (Windows 98) or Start | Programs | Accessories | Multimedia | CD Player (Windows 95) to use the player software included with Windows.

authentication Many Internet communications require authentication for security reasons. For example, when you connect to your ISP or a network, the ISP or network computer double-checks, or authenticates, your user name and password to make sure that you're a valid user. In other cases, your computer may send or receive a security certificate (also called digital certificate) which will verify that a Web site you're visiting is authentic, not a false Web site to which you've been secretly or fradulently connected. (See also *ISP* and *security*.)

15

auto open Many programs offer some auto open method. Generally, this means you can specify that a particular file should open or a particular macro should run each time you start the program.

AutoCAD AutoCAD has been the leading computer-aided design (CAD) program for years. The AutoDesk company publishes AutoCAD. (See also *CAD*.)

AUTOEXEC.BAT One of the files that a Windows-based PC runs when it boots (starts up). AUTOEXEC.BAT typically gives the computer a few commands that tell it how to start up. It also may reset certain devices, like the sound card, or load behind-the-scenes utility programs.

autosave The autosave feature on an application will save all open files at a specified regular interval. Then, even if your computer loses power or has a problem, you'll lose only a few minutes' worth of work, rather than a few hours' worth. Be sure to turn on the autosave feature in each program that offers it and set it to save every 10 minutes or so.

avatar If you install 3D chat software like Microsoft V-Chat, you can connect to a 3D chat server. Once you're there, you pick an avatar to represent you in the room. That is, you pick a character that you want to look like in the chat room. To other users in the chat room, you *are* that on-screen character. You can then walk your avatar around the room to talk and interact with other avatars. (See also *chat*.)

> You can download V-Chat from http://vchat1.microsoft.com or another 3D chat program, Worlds Chat, from http://www.worlds.net.

AVI The file name extension for Audio Visual Interleave video files. Microsoft developed this format to work with its Video for Windows program.

axis A horizontal or vertical scale (numbered guideline) against which a program charts data. The x-axis runs horizontally along the bottom of a chart. The y-axis runs vertically along the left side of a chart. A third, z-axis, shows depth.

B

background Most computers today can handle multiple tasks simultaneously (multitask). In such a case, the task or application you're currently using occupies the foreground, and the task or application carrying out prior instructions continues operating in the background. For example, if you start sending an e-mail message and then switch to your word processor, the e-mail program continues sending the message in the background. The term background also applies to documents or graphics. You can apply a background color or pattern to many types of files. You also can choose a background color or pattern for simple shapes you draw.

backplane Backplane systems don't use a motherboard. Instead, an adapter card with the CPU and other primary system circuitry plugs into a larger, slotted board called the backplane. Most standalone PCs today don't use the backplane design because it can be more expensive to upgrade. However, some network server computers or other larger systems may use this design. Some users refer informally to the back area of any system, where cables are connected, as the backplane.

Backspace key A keyboard key that deletes the character to the left of the insertion point in a document, spreadsheet cell, or text box in a dialog box.

backup A special type of file that serves as a spare copy for one or more other files. Most leading programs offer a feature that creates a backup copy of a file each time you save it. For example, when you save a Lotus 1-2-3 file named *Budget.123*, 1-2-3 creates a back up copy of the file named *Budget.bak*. You can open the .bak back up file if the original file becomes damaged. Separate backup programs enable you to back up multiple files on a disk or in a folder in a single larger backup file. The process of backing up one or more files is called "performing a backup" or "backing up the system."

backup program A program that can back up multiple files from a folder or disk into a single, larger backup file, sometimes called an archive or backup volume. You typically store the backup volume on a removable disk (like a Zip, Jaz, or SyQuest) or tape backup drive. You must then use the backup program to restore the original files from the backup volume to a location on your hard disk. Backup programs offer a range of helpful features, including the capability to schedule future backups and receive a reminder when you need to back up your files.

Backup (Microsoft Backup) A backup utility program that comes with Windows 95 and 98 (Figure B.1). Backup offers basic backup features, but not the high-end features such as backup scheduling found in third-party programs you can buy. Still, Backup provides the key features you need to create a backup for your Windows system files or any data files you select, when needed. You should back up your Windows system files monthly and before you install any new software. Choose Start|Programs|Accessories|System Tools|Backup in either Windows version to start Backup.

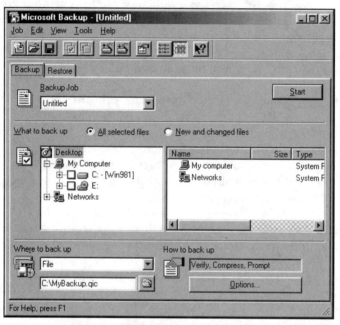

Figure B.1 Use Microsoft Backup (this version comes with Windows 98) to back up your system files and other important files for safety.

.BAK The file name extension typically assigned to a backup file created by the same application used to create the original file. Typically, each time you save the original file, the application updates the .BAK file, too.

bad sector On a hard or floppy disk, a damaged area that can no longer accept data. Normally, your system marks bad sectors so that it doesn't try to write data to them. However, a sector can go bad after the system has stored information in it. In such a case, you can use a utility like ScanDisk, which comes with Windows, or The Norton Utilities to try to get the data from the bad sector. These utilities move the data from the bad sector to another location on the disk. (See also *Norton Utilities* and *ScanDisk*.)

The primary culprits that cause floppy disk damage include metals, magnets, and dust that can damage the magnetized material on the disk media. Even though a floppy's media is encased in harder plastic, damaging materials can make their way in through the sliding metal cover over the opening on one side of the disk. So, keep your computer area clean, and keep metallic objects like paper clips and magnetized objects away from your floppy and other removable disks.

.BAT The file name extension for a batch file. Each batch file holds a series of DOS commands that the system can execute one at a time. This saves you the trouble of typing those commands one after another at the DOS prompt. The *AUTOEXEC.BAT* batch file runs automatically when you start your PC. You can run a batch file by typing its name, including the *.BAT* extension, at any DOS prompt and pressing Enter. (See also *MS-DOS*.)

balloon help A type of help first pioneered in System 7 on the Macintosh where you could point to an item on the screen to see a pop-up balloon with help or information. The current versions of many applications published by Lotus Development Corporation, and some other publishers, include *bubble help*, which is another name for balloon help. When you click on or point to certain items in applications like 1-2-3 and Word Pro, a bubble pops up to give you helpful details.

bandwidth The amount of data a computer component or connection (like a network cable) can handle at any given time. Bandwidth can be expressed in Hz (hertz) or bps, with higher numbers indicating greater bandwidth. (See also *bps* and *MHz*.)

battery pack The battery module that plugs into a notebook computer so you can use it without connecting it to an external power source via an AC adapter cord. Newer notebooks use Lithium-Ion and Nickel-Metal Hydride batteries, which typically can run the system four hours on a single charge. As shown in Figure B.2, you can monitor the amount of power left in the battery. A notebook computer also warns you when the battery is running low.

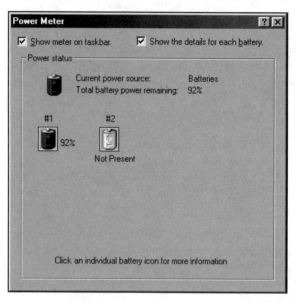

Figure B.2 Notebook computers enable you to monitor remaining battery life.

If you plan to work on the road a lot, make sure you buy a notebook with good battery life. All the bells and whistles today's notebooks offer come with a price—they quickly drain the battery. Some systems even enable you to plug in two batteries at once. Also consider buying a spare battery and an external charging unit, so you can charge up one battery while you're using the other.

baud (see bps)

BBS An acronym for Bulletin Board System, a BBS is an online service set up by an individual or company. Other users can dial the BBS with a modem to exchange messages, read posted information, or download files. BBSs were a precursor for World Wide Web sites, but many BBSs still thrive today because they don't require end visitors to install special software and can offer a clubby or exclusive feel. Some BBSs charge a monthly fee to join, and you often have to dial a long distance number to log on.

beta software Preliminary or test versions of a software program, distributed by the software publisher for testing. With the great interest in computers today, eager users seek out many beta software versions. Be careful with betas, though. Installing a beta can prevent other software on your system from working, so you should always back up your system before installing a beta. Many betas expire after a certain number of uses or after a certain time period.

beta test Software publishing companies may distribute beta software to a number of beta testers (beta test sites). In return for receiving the advanced software copy, each tester agrees to submit detailed problem or bug reports to the software publisher and to participate in online discussions about the beta. Beta testers also agree not to disclose information about the software until the conclusion of the beta test. During the beta test, testers try software on a number of different hardware setups and under a variety of conditions to uncover problems for the software publisher. Prior to the beta test, the software publisher might conduct an internal alpha test.

binary (binary numbers) A system for counting or numbering that uses only two digits, 0 and 1. In a computer circuit, 0 represents the low current, or off state, and 1 represents the high current, or on state. A computer translates the information you enter into a series of 0s and 1s, forming a code to execute a command or store information. In mathematics, the binary system is also called base-2. (See also *bit*.)

BinHex An algorithm used to encode and decode files e-mailed over the Internet. Most e-mail programs and services connected to the Internet no longer require encoding. For example, previously, you had to encode files to send them between the Internet and AOL or CompuServe. Today, encoding happens more rarely. Some corporate e-mail systems automatically encode outgoing file attachments. In most cases, the e-mail message includes the encoded file in the message body, with a header line or two telling you if BinHex or another coding scheme was used. You can use a utility program like Wincode (a shareware program on the Internet) to encode and decode BinHex and other encoded files.

BIOS (pronounced bye-os) The Basic Input/Output System, or BIOS, is a set of read-only programs stored on a chip in your computer. The BIOS performs the POST (Power-On Self Test) and other functions when you start your computer and helps control the hardware connected to the system. In some cases, you have to upgrade the BIOS when you upgrade a system component if the older BIOS doesn't support (work with) all the features offered in the new hardware. (See also *POST*.)

bit One number, or unit of information, in a computer under the binary numbering system it reads. Each bit can be set to either 0 or 1. You'll see the bandwidth for certain system components described in bits, as in a 32-bit bus or 24-bit graphics. The term bit is an abbreviation for BInary digiT. (See also *byte*.)

bitmap A method of displaying information on the screen dot-by-dot. Each on-screen dot (pixel) displays a particular color, based on the setting for one or more corresponding bits of information.

bitmap font A font drawn using a pattern of dots, so that the font isn't scalable. If you try to double the size of text formatted with a bitmap font, the computer in essence increases the size of each dot so that you see unattractive jaggies or a stairstep appearance. Most Windows applications now provide scalable TrueType fonts so you can resize text as you want while avoiding jaggies. (See also *font* and *TrueType font*.)

bitmap graphic Bitmap graphics, like bitmap fonts, consist of a pattern of colored dots. As illustrated in Figure B.3, you often must work dot by dot to edit the image. Because bitmap graphics are built from dots, a bitmap graphic can distort or appear jaggy if you increase its size dramatically. The file name extensions .BMP, .TIF, and .PCX often identify bitmap graphic files. (See also *vector graphic*.)

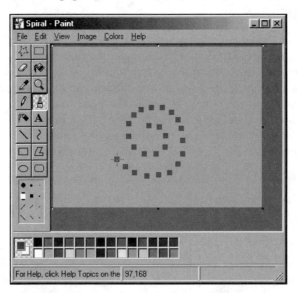

Figure B.3 You can use the Paint applet that comes with Windows to create your own bitmap graphics. Choose Start\Programs\Accessories\Paint to start Paint.

block Some communications software, like Windows HyperTerminal, divides information into blocks to send the information via modem. The transfer method (communication protocol) you select controls the block size. For example, the ZModem protocol uses blocks of 1,024 bytes. You also may use the term block to indicate a selection in a word processor program, as in: "I've selected a block of text."

Computer & Internet Dictionary

.BMP The file name extension for the Windows Bitmap type of bitmap graphic file. You can use the Windows Paint applet to create .BMP files. (See also *bitmap graphic*.)

bold A formatting attribute applied to characters in an application. Making a selection bold (or applying boldface) turns the characters thicker and darker. Bold formatting can be applied to headings and titles in a document to make them stand out from the rest of the text.

bomb out When an application or your PC stops working, it has bombed out.

bookmark In a word processor document, you can mark an area in the document by creating an electronic bookmark. Later, you can select the bookmark to jump to that area in the document. In Netscape Navigator's Web browser, you can create a bookmark to note the address for a favorite Web page. You can then select the bookmark rather than typing the full Web address when you want to display that Web page.

boot To start or power up your computer. When you boot the computer, it performs a number of actions to test the system, such as the POST (Power-On Self Test), and loads the operating system so the computer will be ready to accept your commands. A special read-only memory (ROM) chip on the motherboard typically stores the computer's boot instructions. (See also *bootstrap*, *cold boot*, *POST*, and *warm boot*.)

boot sector The first track (track 0) on the hard disk that stores the operating system software, also called the boot disk. The first block on this track must contain operating system information or the computer will not boot properly.

bootstrap The bootstrap software or bootstrap loader runs as part of the boot process. It checks the boot sector on the boot disk (or any floppy disk you've inserted into drive A) for the operating system software. When the bootstrap finds the operating system software, the bootstrap loads the operating system into RAM so the operating system can take over the PC's operation and accept your commands.

bot Short for "robot," a bot automates particular types of Web or Internet information for you. For example, you can use a bot to perform a detailed search of the Web and to gather all articles or items that match criteria you specify. (So-called search bots or spiders usually charge a fee for this service.) Other bots help you shop. For example, there are bots that can search multiple booksellers' Web sites and tell you which bookseller gives the best price on a book you want to buy. Bots are also called intelligent agents.

bps An acronym for bits per second. It measures how many bits of data per second particular communications software or hardware can send. 56K modems can transfer data at speeds up to 57,600 bps with data compression and other features that increase transfer speed, although phone line capabilities limit actual connection speeds users achieve. The *K* in 56K or *Kbps* stands for *kilobits per second*, about 1,000 bits per second. *Mbps* stands for *megabits per second*, or about 1,000,000 bits per second.

> When referring to disk storage (bytes), the actual number of bytes in a kilobyte and megabyte totals more than an even thousand (1 kilobyte=1,024 bytes) or million (1 megabyte=1,048,576 bytes). However, when you're referring to data transfer speeds (bits or bps), you generally use the decimal meanings for kilo (a round 1,000) and mega (around 1,000,000).

Briefcase A feature in both Windows 95 and Windows 98 that helps you transfer files you want to work on between computers, and then synchronize (update) all copies of the files so they match the file to which you most recently made changes.

browser cache In older Web browser versions (such as Internet Explorer 3.0), the browser cache held copies of downloaded graphics and Web pages. This way your system could quickly redisplay a page you visited earlier without having to download all the page information over again. Newer, browsers refer to these downloaded files as "temporary Internet files," rather than the cache.

> Cached or temporary Internet files can consume a lot of hard disk space. To delete those temporary files and free up disk space, you can choose View|Internet Options in Internet Explorer 4.0, and then click the Delete Files button under Temporary Internet files.

browser software Software that enables you to view graphical Web pages stored on Web sites on the Internet. The browser loads each Web page, complete with graphics and text formatting. You can click linked text, buttons, or graphics to jump to other pages. Or, you can enter a Web page address to go to that page. (See also *hyperlink*, *Internet Explorer*, and *Netscape Navigator*.)

Figure B.4 Web browser software displays graphical Web pages stored on the Internet.

BTW An abbreviation you can type instead of "by the way" in an e-mail message. For example, you might type, "BTW, I received your fax yesterday." You also might see and use other abbreviations like CU (see you) and B4 (before). (See also *IMHO* and *ROTFL*.)

buffer A memory area that holds information before sending it to a device connected to the computer. Typically, the buffer helps dole out information in small quantities to a device that operates more slowly than the rest of the system. For example, a communications buffer routes information to a communication device, while the print buffer holds and feeds data to the printer as fast as the printer can accept that data.

bug An error in a program or macro that causes it to stop working, display an error message, return an inaccurate result, or shows some other operating problem. (See also *beta test* and *debug*.)

bullet A dot, box, check mark, or other small graphic used to set off each item in a list, as in:
- Apples
- Pears
- Bananas

bus A pathway on a PC motherboard that carries information between the parts of the computer. There are several different types of buses in a system. The I/O bus, or main system bus, carries the most information, communicating with all devices connected to your computer, including the disk drives, video card, and printer. Most systems today accommodate more than one type of bus architecture on the data bus; for example, a typical system accepts both EISA and PCI cards (which use the EISA and PCI Local Bus architectures, respectively). Notebook computers also support the PC Card bus architecture, so the system can work with PC Card devices. As another example, the memory bus carries information between the CPU and RAM. (See also *EISA*, *ISA*, *PC Card*, *PCI*, and *VESA*.)

button An on-screen shape you click to execute an action in a program. Buttons may be as simple as a rectangle or oval with text in it, or as fancy as a colored image. You often find buttons in dialog boxes or on a special toolbar near the top of the application window.

byte A group of eight bits of information. Because each bit only represents either a 1 (on) or a 0 (off), computers need a combination of bits to define more complex information. Each byte represents a particular character. A *kilobyte* equals 1,024 bytes, a *megabyte* equals 1,048,576 bytes, and a *gigabyte* equals 1,073,741,824 bytes. (See also *bit*.)

The base-2 math used for bits and bytes results in the actual number of bytes in a kilobyte and megabyte being more than an even thousand (a value identified by the kilo prefix in decimal or base-10 math), million (the mega prefix), or billion (the giga prefix).

C

C One of the first high-level programming languages, developed in 1972. It is "high-level" because C uses English-like commands and statements rather than the more obscure coding used in assembly-language programming. C programs run quickly and are easily portable between Windows-based, Macintosh, and other computing environments. C++ followed, adding the capability of object-oriented programming. More recently, Visual C++ enables the programmer to produce C++ programming in a visual, Windows-based environment.

cable An external connecting wire that carries data between your computer and another device, such as a printer, monitor, network hub, or phone jack. Each cable plugs into a port on the computer. The type of connecting device and the available ports on the computer determine the type of cable needed to make the connection. (See also *parallel cable, port, RJ-11,* and *serial cable.*)

cable modem A modem that sends and receives data over cable television lines, which have greater data capacity than typical phone lines. This communication technology delivers fast Internet connections. To be able to use a cable modem for Internet access, your location must be wired for cable, and the local cable company must offer Internet services to its subscribers.

cache (pronounced cash) A cache works something like a buffer. A cache is a holding area for data within the system. The cache holds information that the CPU needs to access repeatedly. One type of cache is a memory cache. The other type, a hardware cache, works along with the hard disk drive. If you're working with a program where you use a particular command frequently, rather than retrieving that command instruction repeatedly from the disk (a relatively slow operation) the system can retrieve it from the cache (a faster operation). (See also *memory cache.*)

CAD (computer-aided design) CAD programs provide features for drafting industrial, architectural, engineering, and other plans that require tremendous precision. CAD features can include design optimization, statistical calculation, 3D rendering, and symbols to enable the professional drafter to develop and refine highly accurate plans for products and structures. A CAD program typically requires a system with ample speed and processing power (to perform complex calculations) and top-notch graphics capabilities.

calculate To perform a mathematical operation. In most spreadsheet programs, you can manually recalculate the open file so that its formulas reflect results based on the most recent values you've entered.

calculated field In a word processor or database program, a calculated field displays the result of the calculation performed by a formula you previously defined for that field. Typically, the formula in the calculated field references other fields, and uses the data found in those fields to calculate a result. (See also *field*.)

camera-ready A high-quality laser printout (or a printout made using a photographic method), from which a commercial printing company can create film, the first step in preparing a document for a printing press.

Caps Lock key Press the Caps Lock key on the keyboard to begin typing in ALL CAPITAL letters. Press the Caps Lock key again to return to typing in upper- and lowercase letters.

> Most keyboards include an indicator light to tell you when Caps Lock is on. Also note that with Caps Lock on, you still need to press the Shift key to produce certain characters, like !, @, and all other "shifted" characters on the number keys along the top row of the keyboard.

cancel To stop or abort an operation in progress. Often, you can press [Esc] to cancel the command or process. For example, in most Windows applications you can press [Esc] twice to close a menu you've opened (and deselect the menu name) if you no longer want to choose a command from it.

Cancel button A dialog box button you click to close the dialog box without applying your choices in the dialog box. Most dialog boxes in Windows applications, like the one in Figure C.1, include a Cancel button somewhere near the bottom. You also can press [Esc] to close, or cancel, most dialog boxes.

Computer & Internet Dictionary

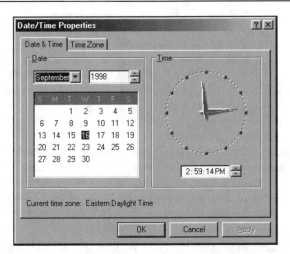

Figure C.1 Click the Cancel button in a dialog box to close the dialog box without applying the choices you made in it.

CardBus A standard for PC Cards (formerly PCMCIA cards) that enables them to transfer data at 100 megabytes per second. CardBus cards are 32-bit cards, while PCMCIA cards are 16-bit cards.

carrier Your modem uses a continuous frequency signal, called a carrier, to move the signal that actually holds your data. The carrier carries the data signal to the destination modem or connection.

cartridge A swappable module that holds, protects, dispenses, or arranges something needed by the computer. For example, you insert a toner cartridge into a laser printer to dispense the toner it prints on pages. Most types of removable drives or backup drives also use some type of cartridge. You insert different disk cartridges into a SyQuest drive or a tape cartridge into a tape backup drive, for example.

cascade To arrange open windows on the screen so that they overlap like a fanned stack of cards, with the title bar for each window visible. You can then click the title bar for any window to select that window. (See also *tile*.)

case-sensitive In some computer environments or online environments, you must enter commands or addresses using exact punctuation. Often, passwords and user logon names are case-sensitive, too. In such an instance, if you assign a password like *TodaY* to a file, you must enter *TodaY* to open the file, not *TODAY* or *today*. As another example, AOL uses case-sensitive Screen Names (user names).

CCITT CCITT defines communications protocols (standards) for transmitting data via modem, serial port, or network.

 Other bodies now define and approve communications protocols. They include the Telecommunications Industry Association (TIA) and the International Telecommunication Union (ITU). However, there are still certain protocols called CCITT protocols.

CD Player An applet in Windows 95 and Windows 98 (see Figure C.2) that you can use to play audio CDs on your computer. To start CD Player in Windows 95, choose Start|Programs|Accessories|Multimedia|CD Player. To start CD Player in Windows 98, choose Start|Programs|Accessories|Entertainment|CD Player. Then insert a CD into your CD-ROM drive, and it will start playing automatically. The control buttons in CD Player look similar to those on your stereo system's CD player and have the same functions.

Figure C.2 Use CD Player to play an audio CD in Windows.

CD-R drive CD-R stands for Compact Disc-Recordable. A CD-R drive can record information to special CD-R discs. The CD-R can only record once to each CD-R disc. Special recording software, usually provided with the drive, helps you organize the information to write before you record, or "burn," the CD-R. You can then use a CD-R drive or CD-ROM drive to read the CD-R disc as many times as you want. Information copied to a CD-R sometimes may be called an "archive."
(See also *CD-ROM drive*.)

Computer & Internet Dictionary

CD-ROM Compact Disc Read-Only Memory disc. CD-ROM discs are about 4.75 inches in diameter and have a polycarbonate wafer coated with a metallic film that holds the data; the wafer and metallic coating together are coated with polycarbonate. One side of the CD-ROM holds printed label information. The metallic coating remains visible through the other side. Each CD-ROM disc holds about 650M of data.

CD-ROM drive A drive that reads—but cannot write to—CD-ROM discs. The CD-ROM drive uses a laser to read the shiny side of the CD-ROM. The laser bounces off *pits* and *lands* in the metallic coating visible on that side of the disc, and the drive reads the reflected light. The reflected light varies in intensity depending on whether it came from a pit or land, and the drive translates each reflection into a data bit that the computer can understand.

Manufacturers reference CD-ROM, CD-R, and CD-RW drive speeds relative to the speed of the early single-speed (1X) CD-ROM drives, which transferred about 150 Kilobytes per second. Thus, a 10X drive transfers about ten times as much data, or 1,500 Kilobytes per second. If you're buying a new system or are upgrading your CD-ROM drive, look for at least a 20X drive, although you also can find 24X, 34X, and even 40X drives. CD-R and CD-RW drives typically work a bit more slowly and generally read data faster than they can write data. CD-R discs can be used for backing up, but each time you create a new backup, you have to use a new disc.

CD-ReWritable drive (also called CD-RW) This type of drive can record to special CD-RW discs multiple times using special recording software. (A CD-RW also can record once to a CD-R disc.) Because you can reuse (record again to) CD-RW discs, they serve as an ideal media for backing up your system. Like CD-R drives, CD-RW drives typically read information faster than they record information.

CD-R and CD-RW drives actually have used a few different formats (standards) over time, so make sure a drive you buy supports all the disc standards you need.

cell The intersection of a column and row in a spreadsheet (worksheet). You can enter text, values, dates, and formulas into each cell. Spreadsheet programs identify each column with a column letter and each row with a row number.

cell address The cell address identifies the specific location of a cell in a spreadsheet (worksheet) using the cell's column letter and row number. For example, the address G15 identifies the cell in column G, row 15.

31

center To position selected information so its center point is equidistant from the left and right margins of a document or the left and right boundaries of a cell or other text box.

central processing unit (CPU) The microprocessor chip that executes commands and controls the data that moves through the computer. The CPU's power defines the capabilities of the PC as a whole. Most systems sold currently use Intel's Pentium II type of processor, although some old Pentium MMX processors may show up in lower-end systems. You can currently buy Pentium II processors that operate at speeds of 266, 300, 333, 350, and even 400 MHz. (See also *AMD*, *Cyrix*, *MHz*, and *Intel*.)

> Intel also makes a processor called the Celeron—basically a Pentium II with some features removed. A cheaper Celeron system may serve your needs if your computing needs are modest or center on basic business computing. However, if you're interested in games, graphics, or CAD, you should always buy the most powerful processor you can afford. That usually means a Pentium II.

Centronics port The computer's parallel port. (See also *parallel port*.)

CGI The acronym CGI stands for Common Gateway Interface. CGI programs are small programs that work with a Web browser and Web server. Basically, when you click a particular button on the Web page, it runs the CGI program on the Web server, and retrieves or otherwise uses the data on the Web server. For example, you might enter product order information into some text boxes (fields) on a Web page, and then click an Order button. The Order button would then run a CGI script to add the information you entered to the order database on the Web server so the Web site's operator can ship your product immediately.

.CGM The file name extension for a Computer Graphics Metafile graphic file, a type of vector graphic format. (See also *vector graphic*.)

channel A channel delivers updated content from a Web site to your Windows 95 or Windows 98 desktop via Internet Explorer 4.0. To receive channel information, you must subscribe to the channel. To set up the channel, automatically download current information from the Web and then disconnect so you can read the information at your convenience. Or, you can set the channel up to update itself regularly. Different channels deliver different types of information, such as news, weather, or travel information. To be able to use a channel for subscribing to a Web site, that Web site must support channels. While some Web sites might divide information into "channels," these aren't automated to deliver information to you like Windows IE 4.0 channels.

Computer & Internet Dictionary

 The term channel may also refer to signal pathways within a computer, such as a DMA channel.

Channel Bar A bar that by default appears at the right side of your Windows 95 or Windows 98 running IE 4.0 desktop (Figure C.3). Use the Channel Bar to find available channels in different categories, and to subscribe to and view those channels. You can also remove the Channel Bar.

Figure C.3 Use the Channel Bar at the right side of the Windows desktop to subscribe to and view channels.

character When you press a keyboard key (or [Shift] plus another key), the specified character appears on the screen. Characters include letters, numbers, punctuation marks, and other symbols.

chart (also called graph) Representing groups or series of data in a graphical form to clarify how values compare or what trends may have developed over time. Most spreadsheet programs and presentation graphics programs offer charting capabilities. You also can insert a chart or graph into a word processor document by copying it from a spreadsheet program into the document. Common chart types include a bar or column chart, line chart, or pie chart (Figure C.4).

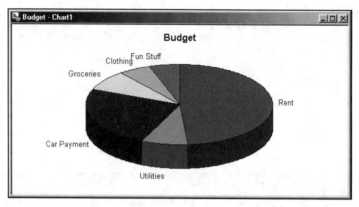

Figure C.4 A pie chart shows you how individual values in a group compare with the total for the group.

chat   To carry on a conversation with others in real time via the Internet or an online service. You enter a chat room and encounter other users. Every message each user types appears on the screen, so that other users can type a response. Chats are an enormously popular online activity.

chat room   A chatting area named according to topic. Chat rooms are designated by name so users can talk with others who are interested in a particular topic. This also enables each online chat site to maintain multiple chat conversations. On the Internet, you'll find most chat rooms on particular Web sites. Or, you can use IRC, a specific type of Internet chatting area that's separate from the Web; on IRC you enter or join a channel rather than a chat room. (See also *IRC*.)

chat software   Special software you must use to chat online. For example, you could install the Microsoft Chat software (it comes free with Windows 98) and use it with Internet Explorer to join chats. You can download other types of chat software from various Internet sites.

check box   A small box in a dialog box that you click to select or deselect an option. When a checkmark appears in the check box, the option is selected. Click the check box again to clear the check box and deselect the option.

Computer & Internet Dictionary

chip A silicon wafer that holds tiny electronic circuitry, the integrated circuit for a computer. A plastic or ceramic covering called the chip carrier typically protects the chip. Protruding pins plug the chip into a socket on the motherboard or other circuit board. The CPU is one example of a computer chip.

chipset A set of one to five chips on the motherboard that hold the main motherboard circuits. The chipset, along with the processor and main system bus, greatly affects the speed at which a computer can operate and what other features (such as type of RAM) it can support. (See also *440BX*.)

choose To pick a command or option in a program. You choose a command from a menu or choose an option in a dialog box. "Choosing" is not the same as "selecting," however. *Selecting* or *highlighting* refers to an action you perform on text or an object in a file. (See also *select*.)

circuit board A board holding the chips, buses, and other connections and components that comprise the circuits necessary to perform particular functions. For example, a motherboard is a circuit board. So is an internal modem, or any other adapter. (See also *adapter* and *motherboard*.)

circular reference A formula in a spreadsheet program that mistakenly refers to the cell holding the formula. For example, you can't enter the formula =SUM(B3:B10) in cell B10, because the formula can't add its own formula result into the formula. More complicated circular references also can occur between formulas. Most spreadsheet programs display an error message if you create a circular reference, and some also provide auditing or other features to help you find and correct circular references.

clear To remove the selected text or object from a file, usually by pressing [Delete] or choosing Edit|Clear in a program. Note that clearing information does not place it on the Clipboard. (See also *Clipboard*.)

click To move the mouse pointer over an on-screen item and then press down and release the left mouse button once.

client application In a networked environment, an application installed on one of the workstations connected to the server, so that only the workstation can run the program. In object linking and embedding (OLE), the client application holds an embedded object from another application. (See also *OLE*.)

35

client/server network A type of network in which client computers connect with a central server computer that holds resources the client computers can share. The server computer typically offers centralized file storage, printers, and perhaps an Internet connection.

clip art Predrawn artwork that you can insert into your files. Most major word processors include clip art. (Figure C.5 illustrates clip art that comes with Microsoft Word.) You also can buy clip art collections from other resources or download clip art from the Internet.

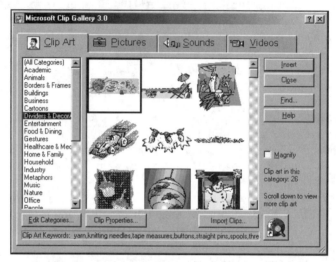

Figure C.5 Many applications offer a collection of clip art images that you can use to enhance your documents.

Clipboard In Windows, a holding area in memory that stores information you cut or copy from a file using the Edit|Cut or Edit|Copy command. You can then paste the information from the Clipboard into another location in the same file or into another file altogether using the Edit|Paste command.

clock An internal clock circuit that generates regular pulses spaced at small intervals. Each pulse represents a single cycle in the system. The computer uses the pulses to synchronize the CPU's activities and information flow in the computer.

clock speed The speed at which a device's clock operates, measured in millions of cycles per second, or MHz. Clock speed usually refers to the CPU's speed. You can roughly compare CPU speeds by comparing the processor speeds; a 300 MHz Pentium II system generally runs faster than a 266 MHz Pentium II system. However, other factors such as the motherboard design and speed also affect how fast computers with comparable CPUs operate.

close To use a command to remove a file or program from the computer's screen and thus from the working memory (RAM) for the system. Closing a file or application frees up RAM so the computer can use it for other purposes. To close a file in an application, choose the File|Close command. To close an application, choose File|Exit. Note that if you haven't saved all your work when you close a file or program, a prompt will appear to remind you to save your work.

Close (X) button One of three buttons at the right end of the title bar for a file window or application window. The Close button has an X on it. You can click the Close button to close the file or application window.

cluster A group of two or more sectors on any computer disk forms a cluster, also called an *allocation unit*. Clusters are the basic units that computers use to store and read data; that is, the computer can't read and write to individual sectors, but it can read and write to clusters. A FAT (File Allocation Table) lists the clusters that hold the information for each file saved on a disk. Because a file may be stored in noncontiguous clusters on a disk, the FAT serves an important function in helping the system find all the disk clusters holding data for a particular file.

When a system recognizes smaller clusters, it can pack more information onto a disk. Older versions of Windows and DOS could only recognize 8K clusters under what was called the FAT16 file system. With Windows 95, OSR 2, and Windows 98, you optionally can use the FAT32 file system, which uses 4K clusters and can pack 10–15 percent more information onto your hard disk.

CMOS (pronounced sea-moss) A computer system's CMOS (Complementary Metal-Oxide Semiconductor) chip tracks basic system setup information, such as information about the hard drive, CPU, and the date and time. A small battery within the system powers the CMOS. Other types of devices may use CMOS chips to store essential information because CMOS chips consume very little power.

coaxial cable A type of cabling with an insulated wire at the center, encased by a solid or mesh metal wire, and finally wrapped in an external insulating shield. Because coaxial cabling can carry a high amount of data (much more than telephone wires), it's frequently used in computer networking, cable television, and cable modem data transmission. For example, Ethernet networks typically use coax (coaxial) cable. In addition, due to its heavy insulation, coax reduces interference during data transmission.

code To write a computer program or macro, as in: "I coded a new game program in Visual Basic."

cold boot To restart a computer by turning the system unit and all its peripherals off, pausing to ensure they power down, and then turning on the power switch for the system unit and peripherals. (See also *warm boot*.)

collapse When you're working with the folder tree in a Windows Explorer window, collapsing means hiding all the folders and files stored within a particular folder. When you're working with the outlining feature in an application, collapsing means hiding all the subheadings and body text falling under a particular heading. (See also *expand*.)

color depth The number of colors a video card can display on the monitor (the video card generates the colors). Most video cards can display in a few different color depths, including 8-bit (256 colors), 16-bit (High Color), and 24-bit (True Color). (See also *High Color* and *True Color*.)

 To change the number of colors displayed in Windows 95 or Windows 98, right-click the desktop and click Properties in the shortcut menu. Click the Settings tab, choose another setting from the Colors drop-down list, then click OK. You may be prompted to restart the system or confirm the color change.

column In a table in a word processor or Web document, a column is a vertical block of cells spanning the whole table height. In a spreadsheet program, a column represents each vertical group of cells. As shown in Figure C.6, spreadsheet programs identify columns using column letters. (See also *row*.)

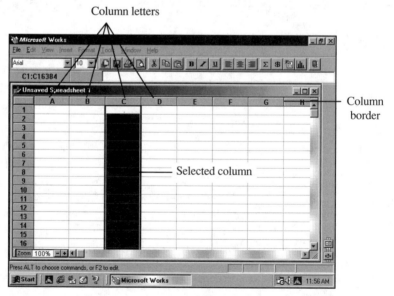

Figure C.6 Spreadsheets organize information in columns and rows of cells.

column border A decorative boundary applied around a column in a word processor table, Web page table, or in a spreadsheet program. In a spreadsheet program, the column border also means the dividing line between column letters at the top of the spreadsheet. You can usually drag the right column border for a column in a spreadsheet to resize the column.

.COM The file name extension that identifies a program command file.

COM port A serial communications port on a computer system. PCs can have up to four COM ports, identified as COM1, COM2, COM3, and COM4. You typically plug your mouse and external modem into a COM port, although other devices may use COM ports, too. (See also *serial port*.)

comma-delimited A plain text or ASCII file in which you type a comma to separate items of data in each row, as in: *Smith, Jane, 222 Any Street, New York, NY, 10000*. When you import the comma-delimited file into a spreadsheet or database program, the spreadsheet or database program can divide the data up into cells or field. Each comma marks the end of the information for a cell or field.

command line (see DOS prompt)

command (also called menu command) An instruction you give to a program to tell it what action to perform. Windows-based applications organize commands on menus. Click the menu name to open it, then click the command you want. Some commands display a dialog box requesting more information, while other commands may display a submenu with further command choices.

command button In a dialog box, a button you click to carry out an action. If the command button name includes an ellipsis (...), the command button displays another dialog box. Most dialog boxes include an OK button, which you click to close the dialog box and apply your choices from the dialog box. The Cancel button in a dialog box closes the dialog box without applying your choices.

COMMAND.COM The command processor file allowing the computer to execute commands that must load when your computer boots.

communications program Any program that enables a computer to communicate with another computer, either via phone lines or a network. In its more narrow sense, this term applies to programs like HyperTerminal in Windows 95 and 98, which you generally use to connect via modem and phone line with another single computer or with a BBS to download and upload files. (See also *BBS*.)

communications protocol Any standard that specifies how computers transfer data over phone lines or over a network. For example, the Internet relies heavily on the TCP/IP protocol. If you're using a communications program like HyperTerminal, you might need to select a protocol like Kermit, Xmodem, or Zmodem. For connected computers to communicate correctly, both or all of them must be using the same communications protocol. (See also *TCP/IP*.)

compact In some e-mail programs, such as Eudora Pro, the compact feature enables you to remove unused or wasted space in a mailbox after you delete messages from the mailbox.

compatibility Refers to whether computing components or software can work together. For example, if you want to replace your video card but don't want to replace your monitor, you need to make sure the new video card works correctly (is compatible) with the old monitor. Otherwise, you must select a new, compatible monitor, too.

composite video A television broadcast method that combines the color signals with vertical and horizontal signals that synchronize the picture. If you have a TV tuner card in a PC and want to output the TV signal from the PC to a television rather than a monitor, you may have to plug into a composite video socket on the television. Many older TVs, however, do not have a composite video connection.

compress To use a special utility program to reduce the amount of space a file occupies. Compressed files take up less space and transfer more quickly over the Internet or a network. Typically, you compress multiple files into a single compressed file. For example, you can compress 10, 100K files (1M of data) into a single file that might only take up only 300K. (See also *WinZip*.)

 You can download shareware compression utilities like WinZip from the Internet. You can get WinZip at *http://www.winzip.com*.

compressed file Also called an *archive*, this is a "container" file that typically holds the contents of several files. It is created using a compression utility. You extract the original files from the compressed file (decompress the file) using the compression utility. The file name extension for the compressed file depends on the compression format and utility used. For example, the WinZip program creates .ZIP files and the LHArc utility creates .LHA files. However, some compressed files are self-extracting and have an .EXE extension. Such files do not require the compression utility; you simply double-click the file in a My Computer or Windows Explorer window to decompress the file.

CompuServe The second largest online service. Even though America Online now owns CompuServe, it operates as a completely separate service with a separate subscriber base, separate software (see Figure C.7), and separate "channels" of information.

Figure C.7 The startup page for CompuServe.

computer A device, usually electrically-powered, that accepts data input, performs calculations, and carries out other operations based on instructions from a human operator.

computer-based training Interactive training programs presented on a PC. Some computer-based training programs require no instructor. The trainee interacts with the program to watch on-screen demonstrations, answer questions, and practice skills. The trainee can work at his or her own pace, back up, and repeat portions of the training, as needed.

CONFIG.SYS The CONFIG.SYS file is read when a computer boots. It loads device driver files that enable the operating system to work with particular devices (like the CD-ROM drive). It also specifies other operating parameters for the system.

configure To change settings for a piece of hardware or software so that it works correctly when you first install it, or so that it works as you prefer at a later time. For example, after adding more RAM to your system, you need to reconfigure a setting for the system to ensure that it can find all of the new RAM.

connectivity The networking and online capabilities of a particular system, based on its hardware and software.

context menu (see shortcut menu)

context-sensitive help Help that addresses a particular on-screen item or operation. For example, in many applications, you can press [Shift]+[F1] and then click an on-screen item to receive information on that item. In other instances, you can open a help feature (called the Office Assistant in Office 97 applications or Ask the Expert in Lotus SmartSuite applications) and then type in a question to see a range of related help topics.

Control (Ctrl) key A key you press in combination with other keys to perform a command or make a selection in an application. For example, in recent versions of Microsoft Word, you can press and hold the [Ctrl] key and click a sentence to select the whole sentence.

Control menu The menu that opens if you click the small icon to the left of the application name or file name in a window title bar. The Control menu contains commands for working with the window. For example, if you click the Close command on the Control menu, Windows closes the window.

Control Panel An area in Windows that you can use to change Windows settings and hardware settings. For example, double-click the Modems icon in the Control Panel to display a dialog box where you can change the settings your modem uses for online connections or install software for another modem. To open the Control Panel, choose Start|Settings|Control Panel in Windows 95 and 98.

controller A separate circuit that operates a full device like a disk drive and manages the flow of information between the device and the CPU.

conventional memory (base memory) The first 640K of RAM, which under MS-DOS was the only area of memory that programs could access (the next 384K out of the first 1M was reserved for MS-DOS system files). Newer systems and programs can address RAM above 1M much more easily, so these systems typically come equipped with 32M or more RAM.

convert To translate information from one format to another so that another device or program can understand it. For example, you can convert a graphics file from .PCX format to .GIF format to include the graphic on a Web page. (.GIF and .JPG graphics work best on Web pages.)

cookie A plain text (.TXT) file that a Web site sends to your system while you're online. The cookie might contain such information as an ID assigned to you by the Web site or preference information you specified while working on the Web site. When you revisit the site, it can read your cookie to recall your preferences or count how often you've visited the site.

> Some users consider cookies a security risk. After all, when you accept a cookie, you're letting some unknown entity save information on your hard disk. Recent Web browser versions enable you to specify whether to accept cookies on your system. In Internet Explorer 4.0, you can right-click the Internet Explorer icon on the desktop, and then click Properties. Click the Advanced tab, and scroll down the list. Under Security, click an option button to choose whether to *Always accept cookies*, *Prompt before accepting cookies*, or *Disable all cookie use*. Then click OK to accept and apply your cookie setting.

coprocessor A separate processor that works along with a main processor. The coprocessor performs a specific function, speeding up the system as a whole. For example, the Intel 486DX CPU included a math coprocessor. The math coprocessor handled heavy-duty calculations to speed up applications that relied on math, like spreadsheet programs.

copy To duplicate selected text, selected cells, or a selected object, typically using the Edit|Copy command or copy button. (See also *Clipboard* and *paste*.)

copy protection A feature in software that prevents non-paying users from installing or using it. For example, a program might require that you enter a certificate number or user number from the original software CD-ROM. Companies that distribute software or shareware over the Internet use other copy protection methods. Some software publishers only let you download a partial or demo version of the program. After an introductory period expires, the software either won't start or flashes a message to remind you to purchase the full version of the software.

43

cps The acronym for characters per second. Cps was typically used to compare speeds for older printers, such as dot-matrix printers. Laser and inkjet printers compare the ppm measurement to gauge each printer's speed (pages per minute). (See also *ppm*.)

CPU (see central processing unit)

crash When a computer or program stops working or "locks up." If Windows itself crashes, it may display a blue screen that tells you the system or application can't work properly. In such a case, you can usually press [Ctrl]+[Alt]+[Delete] to reboot. If the keyboard and mouse have stopped responding, however, you must perform a cold boot to restart. (See also *cold boot*.)

criteria Information you specify when performing a search or query in an application. The search then finds document information that matches your criteria. For example, in an address database, you can perform a query that finds all records with "NC" in the "State" field.

cross-hair pointer A mouse pointer that appears after you select a command or button for inserting an object (like a chart) or drawing a shape in an application (Figure C.8). Drag the cross-hair pointer to define the approximate size, shape, and position for the object.

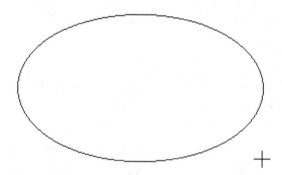

Figure C.8 Use the cross-hair pointer (the small plus) to draw or define a boundary for an object.

Ctrl+Alt+Delete A keyboard combination you press to warm boot the computer. (See also *warm boot*.)

current cell or selection In a spreadsheet program, you click a cell to make it the active cell. If you drag to select a group (range) of cells in a spreadsheet or database table, text in a word processor, or an object in any kind of application, the selection becomes the current selection. Any command or formatting you specify next applies to the current selection.

current file The active file that's ready to accept the next information you type or command you give. The current file holds the insertion point or current selection.

customize To customize an application, you choose options to control whether certain features are available and to specify the defaults for certain settings. For example, you might specify whether or not scroll bars appear in the application window or whether or not the application creates a backup copy each time you save a file.

> In most applications, you can use the Options or Settings command to find customization settings. Look on the Tools menu for this command.

cut To remove a selection from a file and place it on the Clipboard using the Edit|Cut command or Cut button. You can then paste the cut selection to another location using the Edit|Paste command or the Paste button. (See also *Clipboard* and *paste*.)

Cyberspace The vast online world where users interact and exchange information without physically meeting.

Cyrix A company that produces CPUs. Cyrix competes with Intel and AMD. Like AMD, its CPUs often cost hundreds less than a relatively comparable Intel processor. Cyrix presently offers the 233 MHz MediaGX MMX enhanced processor. In conjunction with IBM, it offers the IBM/Cyrix PR233 Processor. (See also *central processing unit, Cyrix, Intel,* and *MMX*.)

D

data Information you enter into a computer. You can then use the computer to store or manipulate the information.

data bus The electronic pathway that the CPU uses to send and receive information.

data compression When a modem sends information, it compresses data to improve transmission speeds, thus reducing transmission time. A modem also must decompress data it receives. Modems use compression protocols such as V.42bis to define how to compress and decompress data. (See also *CCITT* and *V. protocols*.)

data encryption A complex algorithm that rearranges or scrambles information so a third party can't read it during its transmission over the Internet or a network. (See also *decrypt/decryption* and *encrypt/encryption*.)

database A file that holds an organized list of information. For example, a database might list all your audio CDs. The database file divides the list into records and fields. The user could sort the list to find a particular record (CD) listed in the database. (See also *field*, *query*, *record*, and *sort*.)

database program A program you can use to compile and manipulate databases (database files). A *flat-file database program* builds and manages simple database files. Each file in a flat-file database program remains independent; you can't query more than one database at once. The Microsoft Works database tool operates as a flat-file database program. *Relational database programs* allow you to perform more complicated database operations. A file for a relational database program can hold multiple database lists or tables. You can then find and extract information from more than one list at a time, as long as each list has one piece of information (field) in common. Microsoft Access and Lotus Approach both function as relational database programs.

Date/Time The icon in the Windows Control Panel that you use to reset the actual date and time displayed at the right end of the Windows taskbar. (See also *Control Panel*.)

47

dBASE A once-leading database program. Many database and spreadsheet programs can import (read) and export (write) files in dBASE format, so it remains an important database file format.

DDE Dynamic Data Exchange (DDE) was one of the first methods developed to enable applications to exchange data. Although many applications now employ the more user-friendly OLE method for exchanging data, DDE still applies in some instances. For example, the mail merge feature in some word processors uses DDE to find information from a database file and insert that information into the merge document. With DDE, the client application receives information requested from the server application. (See also *OLE*.)

debug Finding and fixing errors in a program. Many programming applications help the programmer find bugs. For example, a program can perform a test run on an application in Visual Basic. Visual Basic stops when it encounters an error to give the programmer the opportunity to note or correct the error.

decimal The point or period (.) that marks the beginning of the fractional portion of a value. In a spreadsheet program, you can control how many decimal places (digits) display to the right of the decimal point. In a word processor, you can set decimal tab stops to align numbers on different rows so that all the decimal points align neatly.

decode To covert a UUencoded or encoded file with another algorithm like BinHex or BASE64 when sent via e-mail. Decoding converts the file encoded with these 7-bit encoded file formats back to its original 8-bit binary file format (.DOC, .EXE, .GIF, and so on). The received encoded file either arrives as a file attachment that has the file name extension for a particular type of encoded file, or it comes within the body of the e-mail message with a message header that identifies the encoding format. (See also *encode*, *.UUE* and *WinCode*.)

decrypt/decryption The act of reversing the encryption process so that you can read a message or file scrambled with data encryption. (See also *data encryption* and *encrypt/encryption*.)

dedicated file server The computer that holds the networking software and central file storage area for a local area network. (See also *LAN*.)

default The initial or normal setting for a feature or object. For example, most software prints one copy of a file unless you change the default and specify that it should print more than one copy.

default folder The folder in which an application saves files or looks for files to open, unless you specify another folder.

defragment When you save a file to disk, the disk drive attempts to write all the information in the file to contiguous clusters on the disk. Over time, as you delete and add files on the disk, the groups of contiguous clusters become smaller, and sometimes the drive has to store different parts of a file in non-contiguous clusters, which fragments the file. The more fragmented files a disk holds, the slower the disk runs. You can run a defragmenter, a utility that reorganizes the information on a disk until every file spans contiguous clusters, enabling the drive to retrieve files more efficiently. Windows 95 and 98 come with a defragmenter called Disk Defragmenter (Figure D.1) Choose Start|Programs|Accessories|System Tools|Disk Defragmenter to start the program. (See also *cluster*.)

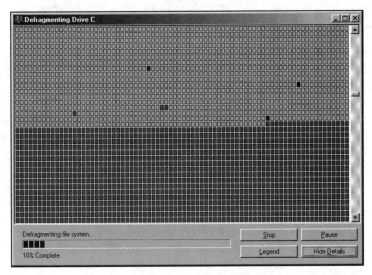

Figure D.1 Use the Windows Disk Defragmenter utility to rearrange file information on a disk into contiguous clusters.

delete To remove selected information from a file, usually by pressing the [Del] key or choosing Edit|Clear. Deleting information does not place it on the Clipboard. (See also *clear*.)

Del (Delete) key The keyboard key that you press to remove a selection from a document.

delimiter In a plain text (ASCII or .TXT) data file, the character or keyboard key that you press to separate each field entry on a row (or record). (See also *comma-delimited* and *tab-delimited*.)

demote To bump a selection to a lower outline (heading) level using the outlining feature in a program.

descender A descender appears on certain lower-case letters, such as g, p, q, and y. The descender consists of any part of the letter that stretches below the main body of the letter. For example, the vertical line that stretches below the loop in a p or q is the descender for those letters. Descenders help make lowercase letters easier to read, by providing greater variation in letter shapes. (See also *ascender*.)

descending order Text information alphabetized in Z to A order or numbers ordered from the largest value to the smallest.

deselect To remove the check beside a dialog box check box. Or, to click outside selected text, cells, or an object in a document to remove selection highlighting or sizing handles.

Desktop In Windows, the working area or screen background that holds the taskbar, icons, and program windows.

desktop computer A personal computer (PC) meant to be used at a desk or other stationary location. A desktop computer usually consists of a relatively large system unit, monitor, and keyboard. (See also *notebook computer*.)

desktop publishing (DTP) Creating publications that integrate text and graphics—typically brochures, newsletters, annual reports, and sales flyers—on a computer. While most word processors offer at least limited DTP features, such as the ability to insert graphics, rules, and other design elements in a document, precise work calls for a separate desktop publishing application such as Microsoft Publisher, QuarkXPress, or Adobe PageMaker.

destination A location to which you copy or move a selection, or a disk to which you copy or move a file.

device Internal or external hardware components that can send and receive data. Devices include modems, printers, disk drives, and sound cards. (See also *peripheral*.)

device driver A program that CONFIG.SYS loads when your system starts. Each device driver remains in memory to control a particular device. For example, the CONFIG.SYS program might load a device driver that enables the system sound card to operate.

diagnostic program Any utility program you run to check the performance of your system hardware or a particular piece of software. Network

Computer & Internet Dictionary

administrators often use diagnostic programs to make sure data is flowing smoothly over a network.

Dial-Up Networking This feature in Windows 95 and 98 enables you to store connection information for dialing a network or Internet connection. You can create a Dial-Up Networking connection to dial your ISP and connect to your Internet account. (See also *Internet* and *ISP*.)

dialog box If you choose a command with an ellipsis (...) after its name, the command displays a dialog box. The dialog box presents options or choices that you make to control what the command does. Figure D.2 shows an example.

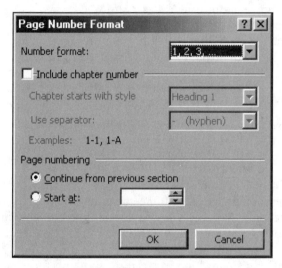

Figure D.2 A dialog box gives you choices for completing a command, in this case formatting page numbers.

digital camera A camera that saves a still image directly to digital format. You can transfer the images from the digital camera to a PC. Then, as with any other graphic file, you can insert the picture file in a document, print it with a color printer, or include it on a Web page. If you don't have a digital camera, you have to scan a picture with a scanner to convert it to a digital image. (See also *digital video camera* and *scanner*.)

digital certificate Electronic information transferred on the Web to verify identity. You obtain a personal certificate by applying with several different Certificate Authorities on the Web. When you connect with a secure Web site, the site checks your certificate to verify your identity. Web sites may have Web site certificates. When you connect with such a site, your browser

51

checks its certificate; the browser warns you if the site's certificate has expired, so that you can double-check the site's address and ensure its securtity. (See also *authentication*.)

Digital Signal Processor (DSP) A high-speed chip on a sound card that enhances the sound card's performance.

digital video camera A camera that saves moving images in a digital video format. As with digital still images, you can use your PC to enhance and edit digital video. (See also *digital camera*.)

DIMM DIMM (Dual Inline Memory Module) memory modules hold RAM. Each DIMM plugs into a 168-pin socket on the motherboard and can hold about twice the amount of RAM as a SIMM. (See also *SIMM*.)

dimmed When a command or dialog box appears grayed out, it's dimmed. You cannot choose a command or option that is dimmed.

DIP switch A small switch in a plastic case called a Dual Inline Package. You change the position of a DIP switch to configure a setting on a circuit board, typically a motherboard or modem in a PC.

Direct Cable Connection A Windows 95 and 98 utility that you can use to connect two computers directly via a null-modem serial cable or certain types of parallel cables. One computer functions as the host, and the other as the guest. Set up a disk or folder on the host computer as a shared disk or folder. Then, when you start Direct Cable Connection, the guest computer can copy files from and save files to the shared folder. You can use Direct Cable Connection to create a private peer-to-peer network, transferring information online between the computers more quickly than you could by disk.

directory (see folder)

Direct Memory Access (DMA) A special channel that transfers information directly between RAM and a device such as a disk drive, so that the information doesn't have to pass through and bog down the CPU. A DMA controller chip moves data through the DMA channel.

disk One of many types of rewriteable magnetic media that holds files created by computer applications. A disk drive reads information from and writes information to the disk. (See also *floppy disk, hard disk,* and *removable disk*.)

Computer & Internet Dictionary

Disk Defragmenter (see defragment)

Disk Operating System (DOS) The basic set of programs and commands that run a computer. All other programs run "on top of" the disk operating system. Most personal computers today use the Windows 95 and 98 operating systems, which integrate the older MS-DOS disk operating system. (See also *MS-DOS* and *operating system*.)

disk partition A section on a hard disk set up to appear as if it's a separate hard disk. You generally create multiple partitions if you want to install multiple operating systems on the same computer. For example, you can install Windows 98 on one partition and Windows NT on another.

 The easiest way to create a new partition on a disk or to switch between partitions is by installing a special partitioning utility program like Partition Magic. A program like Partition Magic is cheaper and faster than installing a second (physical) hard disk. Many online catalogs like *www.egghead.com*, *www.pcconnection.com*, and *www.warehouse.com* carry Partition Magic.

display (see monitor)

dithering To create other colors by combining colors or creating shades of gray from black and white. Dithering also involves shifting dot patterns to adjust the perceived shade. A monitor or printer uses dithering when it cannot produce a needed color or shade. A dithered image can appear chunky where dots clump up.

.DLL The file name extension for a Dynamic Link Library file. Each .DLL file essentially functions as a module of Windows, or different Windows applications, and performs a specific function. When Windows (or an application) needs the function performed by the .DLL, it loads and uses it. When the .DLL finishes, it unloads.

DLP (Digital Light Processing) projector A new technology developed by Texas Instruments that projects images from a monitor onto a large screen for presentations. DLP projectors use a Digital Micromirror Device (DMD), a special chip holding tiny mirrors, to project the image. DLP projectors generally provide a more crisp image than older systems based on LCD technology. In addition, a DLP projector's image doesn't require the lights be dimmed.

53

DNS (Domain Name Server) A DNS server is a computer on the Internet that identifies which domain name, such as www.microsoft.com, corresponds to an IP address that's been requested by another computer. (See also *domain name* and *IP Address*.)

.DOC The file name extension for a Microsoft Word document file.

docking station (also called port replicator) A desktop connection center for a notebook PC. You can plug a full-sized monitor, mouse, and keyboard into the docking station or port replicator and leave them connected. To use those devices with the notebook, connect the notebook to the port replicator. This saves you the trouble of plugging all the individual devices into the notebook itself. The port replicator and the monitor, mouse, and keyboard make the notebook computer feel more like a desktop computer.

document A file created in a word processing program. Web pages also may be called documents.

documentation The instruction books and any online how-to demonstrations that help you use a new PC or program.

domain name The alphanumeric, friendly name for a Web site or other Internet site. For example, home.microsoft.com, www.iquest.net, www.house.gov, www.writer.org, and www.butler.edu are all domain names for Web sites. (See also *Web*.)

> The suffix for a Web sites gives you a clue about what type of organization operates the site. The .com suffix typically represents a for-profit company, while .org usually identifies the site for a non-profit organization. ISPs typically use .net, while .gov stands for a government body's site and .edu stands for an educational entity's site.

dongle A connecting cable that plugs into a PC Card modem on one end and a phone line on the other.

DOS (see MS-DOS)

DOS prompt When you're working in DOS itself (or in a DOS window in Windows 95 or 98), symbols on-screen tell you when DOS is ready to accept your commands. These symbols form the DOS prompt. The basic DOS prompt looks like C:\>, although it will change as you navigate between disks and folders. The DOS prompt can also be called the

Computer & Internet Dictionary

command line. Type a command at the DOS prompt, then press Enter to tell DOS to execute the command.

dot-matrix printer An older type of printer where the print head presses pins against a ribbon to create a pattern of dots on paper in the shape of a letter or symbol. Dot-matrix printers work more slowly and offer lower print quality than inkjet or laser printers.

dots per inch (dpi) The number of dots a printer can print per inch, or the number of dots a scanner can scan per inch, often measured both horizontally and vertically. The higher the dpi, the higher the printout or scan quality the device can produce. For example, a 1200 x 1200 dpi printer creates higher quality output than a 600 x 600 dpi printer.

double-click To move the mouse pointer over an item on-screen and press the left mouse button twice, quickly.

download To transfer a file from another computer to your computer, usually from an online service or the Internet. (See also *Internet* and *virus*.)

> If you're downloading a file from an unfamiliar online source, it may have a computer virus. You should use virus checking software to scan downloaded files for viruses and remove those viruses.

draft A printer setting that prints at less than full quality, providing a faster printout usable for proofreading and checking overall page design.

drag To move the mouse pointer over an object on the screen, press and hold the left mouse button, move the mouse pointer to a new location, and then release the mouse button. You usually drag to move or resize a selected object in an application.

drag and drop A technique where you drag something to perform a command or action in a program. For example, in Windows Explorer, when you drag a file icon from one folder and drop it onto the icon for another folder, the file moves from its original folder to the folder on which you dropped it. In a word processor or spreadsheet, you can drag a selection from one location and drop it into another location to move the selection.

DRAM An older type of RAM called Dynamic Random Access Memory. DRAM costs less to manufacture than other types of RAM due to its relatively simple design.

55

draw program A program that creates vector (object-oriented) graphics. In a draw program, the shapes (objects) you draw remain separate. You can later select a particular object to move it, resize it, or change its formatting. Professional illustrators use draw programs like CorelDRAW!, Adobe Illustrator, and Macromedia Freehand.

drive bay An area in the computer case where you can install an additional disk drive.

DriveSpace A utility program in Windows 95 and 98 (Figure D.3) that enables a disk to hold more information. After you compress a disk with DriveSpace, you have to use DriveSpace to *mount* the disk so that Windows can read it. To start DriveSpace, choose Start|Programs|Accessories|System Tools|DriveSpace.

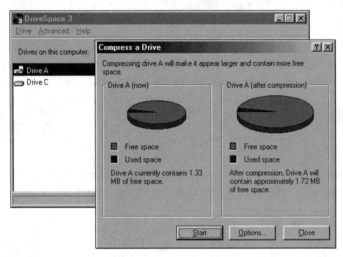

Figure D.3 Use DriveSpace 3 to fit more information onto a disk.

drop-down list A text box in a dialog box or on a toolbar that includes a drop-down list arrow at the right side. When you click the drop-down list arrow, a list of choices opens. You can then click the choice you want in the list.

DSP (digital signal processing) The sound processing function performed by a DSP chip on a sound card.

DSVD DSVD stands for Digital Simultaneous Voice and Data. DSVD enables a modem to carry voice and data at the same time, so you can talk over the modem while transferring a file. (See also *voice-capable modem*.)

duplex (full and half) 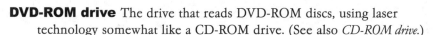 Describes whether a communications device, like a modem, can send and receive simultaneously (full duplex) or can only handle data traveling in one direction at a time (half duplex).

DVD-ROM A Digital Versatile Disc-Read Only Memory disc or Digital Video Disc-Read Only Memory disc. DVD-ROM discs look like CD-ROM discs but hold as much as 17 gigabytes of data. Because they have so much room, DVD-ROMs can hold a full motion picture. (See also *CD-ROM*.)

DVD-ROM drive The drive that reads DVD-ROM discs, using laser technology somewhat like a CD-ROM drive. (See also *CD-ROM drive*.)

E

e-cash A method for paying for services and products purchased on the Internet. Several different companies offer different e-cash schemes. You can "buy" digital cash from an e-cash company like DigiCash. The company gives you one or more e-cash numbers to represent the amount of e-cash you purchased. To pay for a product or service, you provide a number(s). The seller must be equipped to accept your e-cash payment. You can use e-cash in situations where you don't want to transmit a credit card number over the Internet.

e-commerce E-commerce encompasses any buying and selling transaction on the Internet, including shopping for retail goods, purchasing software online and downloading it directly to your system, online securities trading, and business-to-business transactions.

e-mail A message that you send via a network, online service, or the Internet using special e-mail software like Outlook Express (it comes with Windows 98) or cc:Mail. You also can attach a file such as a spreadsheet or graphic to the e-mail message. (See also *file attachment*.)

e-mail address A unique address used to send and route messages to a particular recipient. Different e-mail environments use different e-mail address formats. For example, Internet e-mail addresses combine a unique user name, followed by the @ symbol and the domain for the ISP or company on which the user has his or her e-mail account: *username@isp.net*. (See also *ISP*.)

Easter egg A "bonus" animation or feature hidden in a program by its programmers. The most common type of Easter egg displays a list of all the programmers who worked on the program. Usually, you have to perform a number of unique steps to display the Easter eggs.

 If you have a lot of free time to spend playing with Easter eggs, you can visit a number of Web sites that list Easter eggs. For example, see *http://www.eeggs.com*.

59

ECP/EPP A type of parallel port that supports both ECP (Enhanced Capabilities Port) and EPP (Enhanced Parallel Port) operating modes. Both ECP and EPP ports operate much more quickly than older types of parallel ports. In fact, EPP ports function about 10 times faster than older types of parallel ports. Most new systems have a parallel port that supports EPP, ECP, or both. (See also *parallel port*.)

edit To make a change to information in a file. Many programs offer editing commands on an Edit menu.

EDO RAM Extended Data Out (also called Extended Data Output) RAM, a type of RAM that improved performance by up to 20% over the earlier, non-EDO RAM. EDO RAM comes as 72-pin SIMMs. EDO RAM works well on systems with a bus speed of up to 66MHz. Many new systems today use either EDO RAM or SDRAM. (See also *bus* and *SDRAM*.)

EIDE An ATA-2 (Enhanced IDE) connection used to connect a disk drive to the system motherboard. EIDE enabled PCs to use hard disks larger than 504M. EIDE hard disks also can transfer data at up to 16M per second. (See also *ATA hard disk* and *IDE*.)

EISA The Extended Industry Standard Architecture bus, a type of I/O bus used on 80386 systems that preceded the faster local bus. (See also *local bus*.)

eject To cause a floppy disk, removable disk, or CD-ROM to pop out of the drive. For most drives, you press a button to eject the disk. For CD-ROM drives, you also can click an eject button in most CD software to eject the disk. You also can right-click the CD-ROM icon in the Windows My Computer window and then click the Eject command.

ellipsis (...) The ellipsis (...) appears to the right of certain command names on a menu. When you choose a command that includes an ellipsis, the program displays a dialog box so that you can make more choices for completing the command. Some command buttons within dialog boxes also have an ellipsis beside the button name; clicking this type of button also displays a dialog box where you can make particular choices.

embed In OLE, embedding means inserting an object in one application that you created in another application. For example, you can insert a graph created from Microsoft Graph into a Microsoft Word document. (See also *OLE*.)

Computer & Internet Dictionary

emoticon Sometimes called a *smiley*, this is a combination of characters that you type in an e-mail message or newsgroup posting to create a sideways face expressing your feelings or an action. Smileys can indicate happiness :), sadness : (, a wink ;), a yawn : 0, and so on.

EMS Expanded Memory Specification is a method that a computer can use to access expanded memory. (See also *expanded memory*.)

encrypt/encryption A method of scrambling a message or file so that the recipient needs a special password or special decryption software to read it. Encryption provides greater security for Internet transmissions. (See also *data encryption* and *decrypt/decryption*.)

End key Use the End key to navigate in programs. For example, pressing [End] in a word processor moves the insertion point to the end of a line. You often can press [Ctrl]+[End] to move to the end of a word processor document or to the last cell that holds text in a spreadsheet.

encode When you encode a file, you transform an 8-bit binary file (a file in its original format, like .DOC, .EXE, or .GIF) to use a 7-bit ASCII-based encoded file format, like UU, XX, USR, Base64, or BinHex. Many text-based (ASCII-based) e-mail programs can only work with text-based data, necessitating the encoding process. Some e-mail programs actually encode and decode files automatically, but in other cases you need to manage the process manually with a utility program like WinCode. You also may find encoded information in Internet newsgroup messages. (See also *decode*, .UUE, and *WinCode*.)

Energy Star This is the name for the EPA standard developed to identify power-conserving PCs and peripherals. To be Energy Star-compliant, a PC or component must be able to enter a low power mode, or "sleep" mode, after a period of inactivity (when no user has pressed a key or clicked the mouse). In the low power mode, the computer or component must draw less than 30 watts of power.

 Windows 98 supports new power features called APM or Advanced Power Management for even better power conservation on desktop and notebook PCs.

61

enhanced keyboard Enhanced keyboards include a 10-key keypad to the right of the main group of keyboard keys. Computer users with 10-key skills, such as financial professionals and bookkeepers, can use the 10-key keypad to enter numeric information more quickly. While desktop systems usually come with an enhanced keyboard, most notebook system keyboards typically lack the 10-key keypad.

Enter key Press [Enter] to start a new paragraph in a word processor or finish an entry in a spreadsheet or database table cell. You also can press [Enter] in most dialog boxes to close the dialog box and apply your dialog box selections.

.EPS The file name extension for a PostScript graphics file. PostScript files behave like most other types of vector graphics. However, a printer must be able to work with PostScript to print .EPS files. (See also *PostScript* and *vector graphic*.)

error messages An operating system or application displays an error message (Figure E.1) when a problem occurs or when you request an action that can't be completed. For example, you might see an error message if you enter a spreadsheet formula incorrectly. Usually, the error message includes a description of the problem and gives you options for proceeding.

Figure E.1 Error messages alert you when there's a problem and give you options for how to proceed.

Esc key You press [Esc] to cancel actions, in most cases. For example, if you open a menu in an application, you can press [Esc] twice to close the menu and deselect the menu name. You also can press [Esc] to close an open dialog box without applying your choices in the dialog box. (See also *cancel*.)

Ethernet A hardware, protocol, and cabling standard that defines a particular type of LAN. An Ethernet network can connect up to 1,024 machines, including UNIX, Macintosh, and Windows-based workstations. You can use different kinds of cabling with an Ethernet network, including twisted pair, 10BaseT, and coaxial cable. Standard Ethernet operates at 10 Mbps. Fast Ethernet can transfer data at up to 100 Mbps. (Mbps stands for megabits per second, or 1,000,000 bits per second, of data transfer.)

Eudora Eudora is an Internet e-mail program published by Qualcomm. You can download the Eudora Light shareware version from the Internet at http://www.eudora.com. You also can buy the retail version, Eudora Pro. Eudora Pro enables you to apply attractive formatting to your e-mail messages and provides more features for organizing received messages.

Excel The Microsoft Excel spreadsheet program, also part of the Microsoft Office suite, leads the spreadsheet market. Like other spreadsheet programs, Excel provides many functions that you can use to perform complex calculations. Excel offers additional functions like AutoFormats (see Figure E.2).

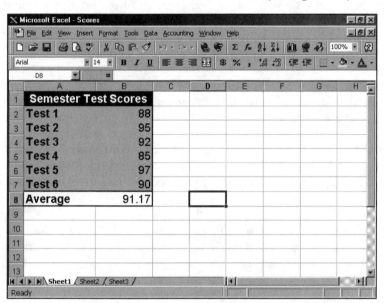

Figure E.2 The Microsoft Excel spreadsheet program enables you to organize and calculate numeric information.

.EXE The file name extension for executable or program files. For example, if you double-click the CALC.EXE file in the Windows folder, the Calculator applet starts in Windows.

Exit The command typically found on the File menu that you use to close a program. The term exit refers to shutting or closing down any application.

expand When you're working with the folder tree in a Windows Explorer window, expanding means redisplaying all the folders and files that have been hidden or collapsed within a particular folder. When you're working with the outlining feature in an application, expanding means redisplaying all the subheadings and body text hidden or collapsed under a particular heading. (See also *collapse*.)

expanded memory A special type of memory, defined by the EMS specification, used by certain DOS programs. The EMM386.EXE memory emulator program can use a 64K area or page of memory in the Upper Memory Area (the area between the base memory—the first 640K—and 1M of memory.) EMM386.EXE sets up part of the extended memory to work like expanded memory, and exchanges 64K of information at a time between that "converted" memory and the 64K page in the Upper Memory Area. (See also *EMS, extended memory, upper memory,* and *XMS*.)

expansion card This is another name for the adapter or card you plug into the system's motherboard. The slots that adapters plug into often are called *expansion slots*. (See also *adapter*.)

expansion bus This is another name for the I/O bus, main system bus, or data bus. The I/O bus carries information to and from the devices (adapters) plugged into the expansion slots on the system. (See also *bus* and *expansion card*.)

extract (also called unzip) To use a special utility program to retrieve an individual file from a compressed "container" file and expand that file to its full, original size. (See also *compress* and *WinZip*.)

extranet Similar to an intranet, an extranet network can transfer and display information in the form of Web pages. The company that owns the extranet lets certain outsiders, such as customers and other business partners, access all or part of the information on the extranet. For example, a company may enable a customer to log on to the extranet to check the status of an order. A user must have an authorized user name and password to log onto the extranet. (See also *Internet, intranet, TCP/IP,* and *World Wide Web*.)

extended memory Extended or XMS memory consists of any memory above 1M (1,024K). Most programs can access extended memory without any special help from the operating system; Pentium systems can access up to 4 gigabytes (4,096M) of extended memory. (See also *EMS, expanded memory, upper memory,* and *XMS*.)

extension The extension appears as a suffix on the file name and consists of a dot (.) followed by three characters, as in .EXE or .DOC. The file name extension enables Windows and Windows applications to identify the file type. For example, if you use the File|Open command in Microsoft Word, the Open dialog box that appears by default displays only files with the .DOC file name extension. This makes it easier to find the file you want, because you see only files of one type. In Windows, the extension identifies the file association. (See also *associate*.)

external drive Unlike an internal drive installed within the case of your PC, an external drive has its own case and connects to the PC via a cable. Some external drives connect to the parallel port. Others may require that you install a special card to make the connection. SyQuest drives and Zip drives come in both internal and external models. (See also *SyQuest drive* and *Zip drive*.)

FAQ This acronym for "Frequently Asked Questions" refers to a list of questions and answers about a topic provided on a Web site, newsgroup, or as a file that comes with software. Experienced Internet newsgroup participants first compiled FAQs (see Figure F.1) as a reference for new users to prevent the same questions from appearing repeatedly on the newsgroup. (See also *Internet*, *newsgroup*, and *World Wide Web*.)

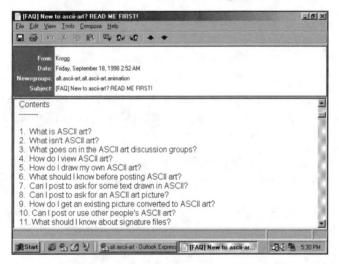

Figure F.1 Look for FAQs (answers to frequently asked questions) on newsgroups (as in this example), on Web sites, and with new software and hardware.

FAT FAT stands for File Allocation Table. This hidden table tracks information stored on each cluster on a disk (floppy, hard, or other removable disk). Because the clusters for a single file may be scattered over a disk rather than in a contiguous block of clusters, the FAT enables the system to find all the clusters to open the file. (See also *cluster*.)

Favorite In Microsoft's Internet Explorer Web browser, you can create a Favorites list to note the address for a favorite Web page. Then, you can select the Favorite rather than typing the full Web address whenever you want to display that Web page. Also, in the My Computer Window of Windows 98, you can add a folder to the Favorites list (menu) to display its contents in the My Computer window.

> To add a Favorite to your list in Internet Explorer or the Windows 98 My Computer window, choose Favorites | Add to Favorites. To display a Favorite page, open the Favorites menu, choose the folder that holds the Favorite, and click the Favorite.

fax software Fax software enables a fax/modem to send and receive faxes. Create a coversheet in the fax software and then attach the file to send. When you send the fax, the fax software tells the fax/modem to dial the fax number specified, send the cover sheet, and send the attached file, page by page. Similarly, faxing software tells the fax/modem to respond to incoming fax calls and store fax pages electronically so you can later view or print them.

fax/modem A fax/modem can send and receive both regular data transmissions and faxes.

> If you plan to travel and receive faxes while on the road, you definitely need a fax/modem. However, if you already have a fax machine on a dedicated phone line, you may not want to abandon it just yet. While you're connected to the Internet, the fax/modem won't be able to receive incoming faxes. So if you're frequently connected to the Internet, it may be best to stick with separate phone lines (and devices) for voice calls, faxes, and modem connections.

female connector The receptacle on a device or on one end of a cable with pinholes. The pinholes accept the pins of a matching male connector. Note that the male connector has to have the same shape and same number of pins as the shape and pinholes for the female connector.

fiber optic cable This type of cable transmits data via glass fibers encased in a covering rather than through wire. Fiber optic cable can carry substantially more data than more traditional types of cable and is less susceptible to interference. Many local cable companies are installing fiber optic cable, both to improve cable delivery service and to enable fast Internet access via a cable modem. Some local phone companies also use fiber optic cable. (See also *cable modem*.)

field In a database, a field represents a piece of information common to all the entries. For example, if you create a database to list all your audio CDs, the fields might be *Title*, *Artist*, *Genre*, and *Price*. (See also *database* and *record*.)

Computer & Internet Dictionary

file A named unit of information stored on a disk. Each application creates a specific type of file. The Word word processor creates document files, each of which has the .DOC extension. The Excel spreadsheet program creates workbook files, each of which has the .XLS extension. You decide what information to enter and save on each file. (See also *associate, extension,* and *save.*)

file attachment When you send an e-mail message or newsgroup message, you can send a particular file with the message (Figure F.2). This is called *attaching* the file or adding a *file attachment*. You can attach document files, spreadsheets, graphics, or any other type of file. The recipient or a newsgroup participant can save the file attachment and open it using any program that handles files of the applicable type. (See also *file size.*)

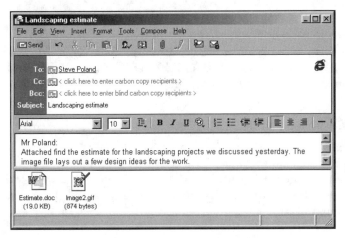

Figure F.2 Each of the two icons at the bottom of this window represents a file attachment.

file name extension (see extension)

file server (see dedicated file server)

file sharing File sharing controls how users share information on a network. For a user to access a particular file on the file server (or another connected computer), the file must be on a disk or in a folder that has file sharing enabled. When you enable the file sharing feature for a disk or folder under Windows or Windows NT, it shares the disk or folder, giving other users access to the files in the disk or folder. If you don't enable file sharing, other users may not view or otherwise use the disk or folder contents. (See also *dedicated file server* and *LAN.*)

69

file size The number of kilobytes or megabytes of information in a file. You may need to know the file size to know if a file will fit on a floppy disk (each standard HD 3.5-inch floppy holds 1.44M or 1,440K of information). You also must consider the file size for any file attachment you send via e-mail. Many ISPs will not send a message with a file attachment larger than 2M. Large file attachments also can bog down e-mail on a company network. (See also *ISP*.)

file window When you open a file in an application, it opens in its own window, called a file window. Each file you open appears in its own window and becomes the current file. (See also *current file*.)

> To switch to another open file (and its file window), open the Window menu in the application with which you're working and click the name of the file you want to use.

fill Many spreadsheet programs offer a fill feature, which lets you copy an entry from one cell across the row or down the column. Also, in many programs, you can apply a fill, or background, to an object you draw, a selected range, or a selected paragraph.

filter A filter limits the information displayed in a list, such as a database list, a list in a spreadsheet, or a list of e-mail messages in an e-mail program. When you apply the filter, you specify the criteria that you want to match, such as a particular e-mail sender's address in the From field of an e-mail message. The list then displays only entries that match the criteria you chose, in this case, all the e-mail messages from the sender you indicated.

find A find operation selects each matching instance of a word or phrase you specify. After the program finds the first matching instance, click a Find Next button or choose a Find Next command to select the next match. Most applications provide some type of find or search capability.

> To start a find, look for the Edit | Find, Edit | Search, or Tools | Find command in your application.

firewall A firewall protects a private network connected to the Internet, such as an intranet. A firewall may be made of hardware, software, or both. The firewall checks outgoing and incoming information (typically e-mail messages and Web page requests) to make sure it meets with established security criteria. The firewall stops unauthorized information from coming into the network, thus preventing such problems as viruses. It also stops unauthorized users from accessing information on the network, thus preventing data theft. (See also *Internet, intranet,* and *TCP/IP*.)

Computer & Internet Dictionary

FireWire (IEEE 1394) ports This new type of high-speed connection enables you to connect up to 63 devices to your computer. Connect the first device to the FireWire port, connect the next device to the first one, and so on in a *daisy chain*. The FireWire ports on new PCs currently can transfer information at 200 Mbps, but soon FireWire ports might handle data at up to 1 Gbps. Because a FireWire port can move so much data, most digital video cameras will likely connect to a PC via a FireWire port in the future. Windows 98 supports FireWire, but Windows 95 does not. (See also *bps*.)

flame Any message that intentionally insults, expresses anger toward, or includes nasty language about another chatter or poster is a flame. You may see a flame in online chat areas and Internet newsgroups.

flash memory card These small removable cards function as removable disks for small devices like digital cameras.

flat panel display This type of monitor for desktop PCs looks similar to a notebook monitor. Because it's less than two inches thick, a flat panel display saves space on your desk. Flat panel displays presently cost about twice as much as standard monitors with a comparable display area, but expect prices to become more competitive.

flatbed scanner This type of scanner offers a horizontal glass surface, much like a photocopier, onto which you lay the item to be scanned. Because the item being scanned remains stationary, these scanners tend to yield better results than handheld scanners, where the scanner is dragged, or feeder scanners, which pull through the item being scanned.

floppy disk A type of rewritable computer storage with its magnetic storage media encased in a 3 ½-inch square rigid plastic case. (Older 5 ¼-inch floppies used a more flexible plastic case, lending the "floppy" name to this type of disk.) Because you can insert and remove floppy disks in the floppy disk drives, floppy disks increase the amount of storage for your system. Most 3 ½-inch floppy disks currently feature high density (HD) capacity, meaning they can hold up to 1.44M of information. Older, single density 3 ½-inch floppies hold 720K of information. (See also *3 ½-inch disk, hard disk, LS-120 disk*, and *removable disk*.)

71

The difference between memory (or RAM) and disk space (or storage) often confuses beginning computer users. Information stays in memory only as long as the computer has power. When you turn the computer off, it loses everything in memory. So, the amount of RAM on a system determines things like how many programs you can have open at one time. The disk space (storage) provides more information permanence. When you save a file to a hard, floppy, or removable disk, the file stays there until you move or delete it. You can open a file from a disk to work with the file later. The amount of hard disk space in a system determines how many files it can store.

floppy disk drive This type of disk drive enables you to insert or remove floppy disks through a slot on the front of the PC. The floppy disk drive writes information to and reads information from any floppy disk currently inserted in the drive. The floppy disk drive includes an indicator light to tell you when it's reading or writing. Never eject a floppy from the drive when the drive indicator light is lit; doing so can damage the information on the disk. To eject a disk, press the button near the drive slot.

floptical This relatively rare type of disk and drive combines magnetic and optical (laser) techniques to read and write information. Floptical disks are the same size as 3.5-inch floppy disks, but hold up to 25M of information. Floptical drives can also read from and write to normal 3.5-inch floppy disks.

flowchart This type of chart, often used in programming, illustrates how a process works using different box styles and connecting lines. Flow charts show how a process branches or proceeds in different directions based on whether the answer to a particular question is yes or no.

flush left, flush right When you align a selection in an application, you align it flush left to line it up with the left margin, left side of the cell, or left side of an object. Aligning a selection flush right lines it up to the right margin, right side of the cell, or right side of the object that holds it. You may see flush left alignment called "align left" or "left align," while flush right alignment may be called "align right" or "right align." (See also *alignment*.)

folder You can divide the space on any disk into named file storage areas called folders. The folders help organize the information on the disk, because you can save files covering the same topic in a single folder. For example, you could create a folder for each of your classes, so that you might have folders named \History 105, \English Lit 210, and \Spanish 102 on your hard disk. (Use backslashes to separate disk, folder, and file names.) You then can save your files for each class to the applicable folder. (See also *path* and *subfolder*.)

folder tree In the Windows Explorer (Start|Programs|Windows Explorer) or any Open dialog box, the folder tree gives a graphic representation of the folders and subfolders on a disk. Click the plus sign beside a disk or folder (Figure F.3) to view the folder's contents. Click a minus sign beside a disk or folder to hide the folder's contents.

Figure F.3 The folder tree at the left side of the Windows Explorer window shows the folders on a disk, in this case, the C: hard disk.

font Traditionally, a font refers to a particular set of characters in a particular size and style, such as the bold Times New Roman characters in the 12-point size. In most applications today, however, the font choice refers more generally to the typeface, such as Times New Roman. After you choose a font from the Font list, you can choose the size and styling seperately.

footer You can create a footer to appear at the bottom of each printed page from a word processor document, spreadsheet file, graphics presentation, or database form or report. The footer might include such information as the file name, date, and page number. Footers and headers help the reader pick up key information about the document from any page. (See also *header*.)

form On-screen forms help a user enter information in a word processor document, database, or Web page. The form presents fill-in fields (text boxes) where you type information, check boxes, and click option buttons to make choices.

format When you format selected text or a selected object, you change settings that control the text or object's appearance. For example, you can change the font, size, or color of text. Or, you can apply a colored border around an object and a fill within it.

formula In a spreadsheet cell, you enter a formula to perform a calculation on the values held in other cells. Formulas resemble mathematical equations. You enter an equals sign (=) to start each formula, then use numbers, cell addresses, mathematical operators, and functions to complete the formula. For example, the formula =(C1*5)+C2 multiplies the value held in cell C1 by 5, then adds the value held in cell C2. (See also *function*.)

forward When you're using browser software to move between different Web pages, you can move forward to redisplay a page you backed up to previously. Usually, you can click a Forward button on the browser toolbar to move forward. (See also *browser software* and *World Wide Web*.)

frame The frame feature in newer Web browser software enables the browser to display a Web page that has multiple boxes, or frames, on the screen. You can scroll each frame independently, making it easier to navigate the Web site and display more information. For example, if you perform a Web search, one frame might display the list of matching pages, while the main frame displays the text of one of the matching pages. (See also *browser software* and *World Wide Web*.)

Freelance Graphics You can buy this presentation graphics program (Figure F.4), published by Lotus Development Corp., as a stand-alone application or as part of the Lotus SmartSuite group of products.

Figure F.4 Use Lotus Freelance Graphics to create colorful slideshows.

Computer & Internet Dictionary

freeware You can download freeware programs from the Internet and other online resources and install and use them for free. (See also *shareware*.)

FrontPage Use the Microsoft FrontPage software to design your own Web pages (HTML files). Windows 98 and Internet Explorer 4.0 include FrontPage Express, an entry-level version of the program.

FTP FTP stands for File Transfer Protocol, a method of transferring files over the Internet. You can use a separate FTP program like CuteFTP to connect to FTP sites. Some Web pages include links to files stored on an FTP site, which you can download to your computer. (See also *download*, *Internet,* and *World Wide Web*.)

function In a spreadsheet program, a function serves as shorthand for a more complicated calculation. For example, you can use the AVERAGE function in Excel to average a list of numbers, rather than building a formula to perform the calculation. In programming language, a function typically returns a value on which the program you're creating can then act.

Function keys Sometimes called F-keys, these keys appear in a row above the numbers at the top of the keyboard. Software publishers use the function keys as shortcut keys for accessing program features. For example, you can press [F1] to display online help in many applications. In Excel, you can press [F9] to recalculate the worksheet. You can press [Alt]+[F4] to exit many programs, too.

G

G (gigabyte) A gigabyte equals 1,073,741,824 bytes of information, or 1,073M (megabytes.)

<g> You can type <g> in an e-mail message or newsgroup posting as shorthand for "grin," to indicate that you're smiling or joking about what you're writing. (See also *emoticon* and *netiquette*.)

> Because e-mail and newsgroup messages can't express your body language and facial expression, it helps a great deal to give your reader(s) clues about the tone and spirit of your message.

game adapter This type of adapter adds a port to your computer where you can plug in a joystick or other game control device. Many PCs come with a game port. (See also *adapter*.)

Gantt chart This special chart type offered in project management software plots out each task as a bar on a calendar. The length of the bar indicates how long it should take to complete the task. A Gantt chart makes it easier to see when tasks start and finish and which tasks are in progress at the same time. (See also *Project*.)

gateway A gateway connects one network to another. The gateway helps connected networks communicate, even if those networks use different networking protocols. For example, a company might use a gateway to connect its Ethernet network to the Internet (the Internet uses TCP/IP, for example). The gateway typically consists of both hardware and software. (See also *TCP/IP*.)

.GIF This file name extension identifies graphics interchange format graphics files. Originally developed for the online service CompuServe, files in this format provide a good image quality despite having a small file size, making them ideal as Web page graphics. (See also *JPG*.)

GIGO The GIGO (garbage in garbage out) acronym reminds you that the results you get from a computer program are only as good as the data you enter. If you make a mistake when you enter a spreadsheet formula, it can't possibly calculate the correct result.

Go To You can use the Go To feature in a program (Figure G.1) to jump to a particular location in the current file. In most applications, you choose Edit|Go To or press [Ctrl]+[G] to start the Go To feature.

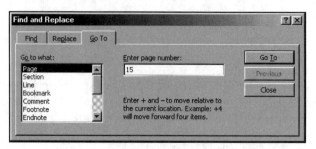

Figure G.1 You can use the Go To feature in a program to jump to a location in a file.

Go word In CompuServe, you use a Go word to jump to a particular CompuServe service. For example, you can use the Go word "ENS" to go to CompuServe's Executive News Service.

grammar checker Top word processing programs can check the grammar used in a document in addition to checking the document's spelling. The grammar checker compares each sentence to a set of grammar rules and highlights any sentence that may violate a rule. You can then decide whether or not to change the sentence.

graphical user interface (GUI) Operating system features that enable the user to communicate with the system by clicking buttons and working with other graphical features, such as windows.

> "GUI" is sometimes pronounced "gooey."

graphics Electronic still images that you can create and display using a PC are graphics, also called graphics files. "Graphics" also refers to a PC's capabilities for displaying graphical images and data. For example, if an ad for a new PC says that it features "AGP graphics," that means it includes special features to improve graphical display. (See also *AGP graphics*.)

grayscale An image using shades of gray in addition to pure black and white to represent shapes and shadows more realistically than a pure black and white image.

gridlines Gridlines separate cells in a spreadsheet, database table, or a table in a word processor document.

H

hacker A hacker uses his or her computer expertise to access private information on a remote computer system via modem. Although one can hack as a hobby or a means of personalizing and improving programs, hackers also have stolen credit card and Social Security information in some cases. Hacking can lead to prosecution and conviction.

halftone A halftone image is a black and white photo prepared for printing. A scanner can create a digital halftone. The scanner and its software convert the continuous shades in the photo to dots of varying sizes. Larger, more dense dots create the darker areas of the image, while smaller, more sparse dots represent the lighter areas. If you were to scan the photo without converting it to a halftone, the resulting image would show more distinctive blotches of black and white and would lack the detail of the original photo.

> You can save a scanned halftone in a number of different bitmap graphic file formats, such as .TIF.

hand-held PC A PC so small you can literally carry it in one hand. Some hand-held PCs offer a small keyboard, but for others, you use a pen or stylus to choose buttons on the screen. The PC can also convert your handwriting to characters. Some hand-held PCs use the Windows CE operating system, a compact version of Windows, while others use a unique interface. Hand-held PCs include the PalmPilot and Palm III from 3Com, the Velo and Nino from Philips, the Sharp Mobilon, and the HP 660 LX.

handle When you chat online or use a newsgroup you can use a nickname, or handle, rather than your real name. A handle can reveal your personality without providing your real name, allowing you to remain anonymous if you prefer.

handles When you click an object in a program, such as a graphic inserted into a word processor document, handles appear at the corners and sides to show that the object is selected. Dragging a handle will resize the object. (See also *select*.)

handshake When you try to connect to another computer via modem or a network connection, the connections exchange signals (a "handshake") to clarify the method of communication.

hard disk The series of magnetic storage platters within a hard disk drive. The hard disk holds the files for the computer's operating system, program files, and files you create with programs. The hard disk serves as a computer's main storage device not only because it can hold so much data but also because it offers more security and protection for the data.

hard disk drive The hard disk drive holds the hard disk platters. Its read/write head reads the information from and writes the information to the sectors on the hard disk. A hard drive holds the disk platters in an airtight case, making the hard disk data less prone to damage than a floppy disk.

Remember, you can't save a file to a "drive," the mechanical device that reads and writes disks. You save a file to a "disk," the magnetic media that holds your data.

hard page break A page break that you insert manually in a chosen location in a document, usually by pressing [Ctrl]+[Enter]. For example, you could insert a hard page break to create a title page in a document, shifting the body information to the top of the next page.

hardware The circuitry and other physical components that make up a PC's system unit and the devices connected to the system, like the printer, monitor, and keyboard. (See also *program*.)

Hayes compatible A modem that's compatible with the modems made by Hayes Microcomputer Products, which was the first leading modem manufacturer. Hayes compatible modems recognize the AT commands. (See also *AT command set*.)

HD (high density) High density floppy disks can hold twice as much data as single density (SD) disks. 3.5-inch HD floppies hold 1.44M of information. (See also *3 ½-inch disk* and *floppy disk*.)

head The head in a disk drive reads data from and writes data to the disk.

header You can create a header to appear at the top of each printed page from a word processor document, spreadsheet file, graphics presentation, or database form or report. The header might include such information as the file name, date, and page number. Like footers, headers give key information about the document on every page. (See also *footer*.)

Help The Help feature in a program explains how to use a feature, provides background information, or supplies definitions. Figure H.1 shows the Help window for Windows 98, which you display by choosing Start|Programs. In most programs you can find a term by topic, by using an index, or by searching for a keyword.

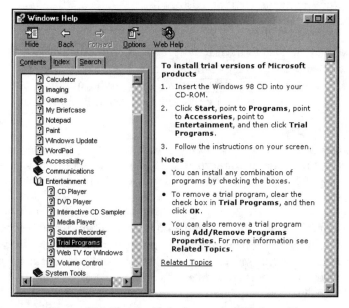

Figure H.1 Use the Help feature in Windows 98.

High Color (16-bit) If your video card and monitor display High Color or 16-bit color, they can display up to 64K or 65,536 colors at a time. (See also *True Color*.)

 To change how many colors Windows displays, right-click the desktop and click Properties. Click the Settings tab. Choose another color option from the Color Palette (Windows 95) or Colors (Windows 98) drop-down list, then click OK.

high memory High memory is the same as upper memory. It is the area of memory between 640K and 1M in the first megabyte of system RAM. High memory is not the same as the High Memory Area, another special memory area where the system can load small system programs. (See also *upper memory*.)

highlight (see select)

hit Each time your Web browser software requests a piece of information (a graphic, a block of text, or a sound file) from the Web server computer, the server registers a "hit." Hits give a Web site a rough measure of its popularity and traffic.

History list By default, your Web browser keeps a list of Web sites you have visited during recent browsing sessions. To return to a site, you can select the site name from the History list.
(See also *browser software* and *World Wide Web*.)

Home key Use [Home] to navigate in programs. You usually can press [Home] in a word processor to move the insertion point to the beginning of a line. You also can press [Ctrl]+[Home] to move to the beginning of a word processor document or to the first cell in a spreadsheet. (See also *End key*.)

home page Sometimes, home page refers to the first page your Web browser loads when it connects to the Internet. More often, it means the main page for a Web site, from which you can connect to other pages the site offers.

host A computer on the Internet providing different services. For example, your computer connects to your ISP's host computer to gain access to the Web or newsgroups. More generically, a host is a computer that provides services to other computers on a network, or any other computer that you dial into using your computer's modem.

hot list This is another name for the list of Favorites or bookmarks you can compile in your Web browser program. Also, some Web sites present a list of new or popular topics that may be called its hot list. (See also *bookmark* and *Favorite*.)

hot spot You can click a hot spot within a graphic on a Web page to jump to a linked Web page. Unlike other graphical buttons on a Web page, hot spots have a more subtle appearance because they are integrated into a graphic image.

.HQX The .HQX file name extension identifies encoded files using the BinHex format. (See also *decode* and *encode*.)

HTML The acronym for Hypertext Markup Language, the coding scheme for creating Web pages. Web browser software can read the HTML coding, convert the codes, and display attractively formatted Web pages. While Web page authors used to have to code Web pages manually, more friendly programs like FrontPage enable users to create Web pages using a method similar to creating a Word processor document, where you enter text, apply formatting, and insert graphics. (See also *browser software, FrontPage,* and *Netscape Communicator*.)

http:// and https:// These are content identifiers appearing at the beginning of an Internet address, or URL. A content identifier tells you to what type of site the Internet address leads. The http:// content identifier stands for Hypertext Transfer Protocol, meaning any site with an address beginning with http:// holds HTML information, or Web pages. The https:// content identifier leads off the address for a secure Web site, possibly on an intranet or extranet. (See also *URL*.)

hub A hub connects devices and computers on some networks, especially Ethernet 10Base-T networks, and passes the data between the connected devices and systems.

hung A hung application or computer has simply stopped responding to commands. In Windows, you can press [Ctrl]+[Alt]+[Delete] to display the Close Program dialog box, click the program labeled as [Not responding], and then click End Task to close the hung application. If the system itself hangs, you need to reboot it. (See also *cold boot, crash,* and *warm boot*.)

hyperlink A link you click to display another Web page or document. Most often, hyperlinks appear in Web pages and can consist of specially formatted text, buttons, and hot spots on graphics (see Figure H.2). Recent versions of top applications also enable you to insert hyperlinks within the files you create or even within e-mail messages. For example, you can insert a link to a Web page in a Word document or even a link to another file on your hard disk; clicking the link displays the linked Web page or file.

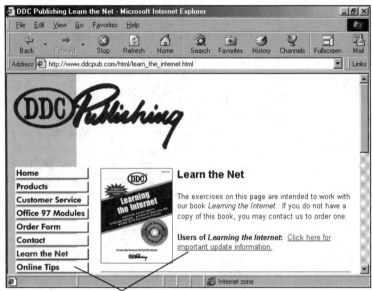

Figure H.2 You can click a hyperlink to display another Web page.

I

I-beam pointer The I-shaped pointer that appears when you move the mouse over the text in a document, a database field, or a text box in a dialog box. Click the I-beam pointer to move the insertion point to a new location in the document. (See also *insertion point*.)

icon These small pictures represent files, folders, programs, and features in Windows and Windows applications. Figure I.1 shows icons on the Windows desktop. Double-click an icon to open the file or run the program. In some cases you only need to click an icon once. You often can right-click to display a menu of commands for working with an icon.

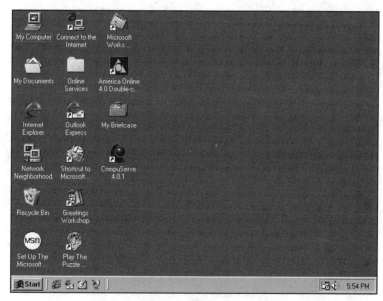

Figure I.1 Icons appear throughout Windows, including on the desktop.

IDE IDE stands for Integrated Drive Electronics, a type of connection between a disk drive (usually a hard disk drive) and a computer. IDE disks use the ATA connection standard; "IDE" and "ATA" are roughly interchangeable terms. (See also *ATA disk* and *EIDE*.)

Illustrator A draw program from Adobe that you can use to create vector (scalable) graphics. Illustrator is the leading professional draw program for both Windows and Macintosh systems. (See also *draw program*.)

85

image-editing software This term describes any program that can edit graphics files, especially bitmap files. This term may also be applied more specifically to programs that can manipulate and convert images from scanners and digital cameras.

IMHO This abbreviation stands in for "In My Humble Opinion" in e-mail messages, online chats, and newsgroup postings.

import To use information from one program in another, completely different program. For example, you might import a Lotus 1-2-3 spreadsheet into Excel, or open an Access database file in Excel. Some programs offer a File|Import command you can use to import files. In other cases, choose File|Open, and then select the type of file to open from the Files of type drop-down list.

inbox The folder in your e-mail program that displays newly received e-mail messages.

indent To set one or more lines of a paragraph in from the left or right margin in a word processor document. If you indent the paragraph's first line from the left margin, you create a first-line indent. If you indent the paragraph from the left margin, except the first line, you create a hanging indent. You can also indent the entire paragraph from either or both sides.

information superhighway A more colorful name for the Internet and other data transfer avenues with which it may eventually connect.

infrared port A relatively new type of wireless port used to transfer information over short distances. For example, you can transfer data between a notebook system and a desktop system or between a notebook system and a printer. Note that both devices must have infrared capability for the transfer to work.

> The acronym IrDA, short for Infrared Data Access, also is used to describe an infrared port on a system or printer.

initialize Your system initializes hardware or software to prepare or reset it for an operation. For example, turning on your printer initializes it to make it ready to receive a print job.

Computer & Internet Dictionary

inkjet printer An inkjet printer prints by spraying ink in tiny dot patterns. Because inkjet technology is less expensive than laser printing technology, printer manufacturers began making color inkjet printers, which spray multiple ink colors to create full-color documents.

insert To add or move text into existing text, or to add a graphic or other object into a document. (See also *insert mode*.)

Insert key The keyboard key you press to toggle between insert mode and overtype mode in a program.

insert mode In a word processing program, you use insert mode to insert new text within existing text at the insertion point. Text to the right of the insertion point moves further right to make room for the inserted text. (See also *overtype mode*.)

insertion point The blinking vertical line that appears in a document, spreadsheet cell, database field, or text box to indicate where the next text you type will appear.

install To copy program files from floppy disks or the CD-ROM onto your computer's hard disk. Most programs include an installation or setup program that handles the copy process, as well as making certain changes that enable Windows to find and operate the newly installed program properly.

Intel (pronounced in-TEL) The company that designs and manufactures the most widely used central processing unit (CPU) chips and motherboard chipsets, enabling personal computers to process program instructions.

interface The commands, buttons, graphics, and other program features on your computer monitor that you use to navigate in a program. The interface also provides feedback, such as the page you're currently working with in your document. (See also *graphical user interface*.)

Internet The worldwide network of computer networks to which an individual PC can connect for communication and information exchange. Users connect to the Internet to send and receive files and private e-mail, find information from online resources, participate in public message and chat areas, and even shop and transact other business, such as stock market transactions. (See also *World Wide Web*.)

Internet backbone The high-speed lines that carry information between large server computers on the Internet. The backbone computers "serve," or control, the Internet by directing traffic (messages or information) to the appropriate points, where it can then be carried to your computer. As large companies enhance the backbone to handle more traffic, the Internet becomes more efficient and faster.

Internet Connection Wizard A wizard offered in recent versions of Windows that easily enables you to set up your computer to connect to the Internet. The ICW creates a Dial-Up Networking connection, which Windows uses to dial and connect to your account with an Internet Service Provider (ISP). (See also *Dial-Up Networking* and *ISP*.)

> To start the ICW in Windows 95, choose Start | Programs | Accessories | Internet Tools. Then click Get on the Internet or Internet Setup Wizard. In Windows 98, choose Start | Programs | Internet Explorer | Connection Wizard.

Internet Explorer The Web browser software published by Microsoft and distributed with Windows 95 (called OSR 2 in its second release), Windows 98, and other Microsoft program bundles. Windows 98 uses version 4.0 of Internet Explorer, shown in Figure I.2. (See also *browser* and *Netscape Navigator*.)

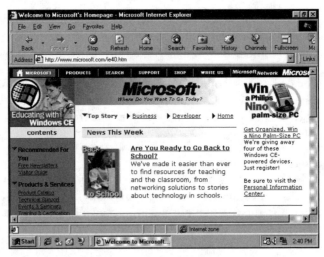

Figure I.2 Internet Explorer 4.0

Computer & Internet Dictionary

Internet Mail An Internet e-mail application often included with version 3.0 of Internet Explorer and Windows 95 OSR 2. With Internet Mail, you can view your list of received messages and a selected message in the same window. Internet Mail has evolved into Outlook Express, an e-mail and newsreader program included with Windows 98 and Internet Explorer 4.0. (See also *Outlook* and *Outlook Express*.)

Internet News An Internet newsgroup reader application often included with version 3.0 of Internet Explorer and Windows 95 OSR 2. With Internet News, you can view posted message headers and a selected message in the same window. Outlook Express in Windows 98 and Internet Explorer 4.0 includes news reading capabilities, eliminating the need for Internet News. (See also *newsreader* and *Outlook Express*.)

Internet Phone Using certain hardware and software, you can make long distance phone calls over your Internet connection, thus saving long distance phone charges.

InterNIC The InterNIC project (which involves AT&T, Network Solutions, Inc., and the National Science Foundation) offers a number of services to Internet users. Most notably, it assigns domain names and IP addresses for Web sites.

intranet An intranet is an "Internet within a company," although it may not be connected to the Internet. If it is connected, the company uses a firewall to prevent unauthorized users outside the company from accessing the intranet information. Intranets are ideal for communicating information to employees, such as new product and inventory information. An intranet network uses TCP/IP like the Internet, so it can present information in the form of Web pages. (See also *extranet, firewall, Internet, TCP/IP,* and *Web*.)

I/O port Any computer port that transfers data into and out of the computer.

IP Address An IP (Internet Protocol) address identifies each computer connected to the Internet, including server computers. Each IP address appears as four sets of 1 to 3 numbers, separated by periods, such as 181.139.245.3. You may have to specify your ISP's IP address when you set up your connection using the Internet Connection Wizard. (See also *Internet Connection Wizard* and *ISP*.)

IRC IRC (Internet Relay Chat) servers on the Internet serve as massive online chat areas. You can chat by logging on to the IRC server of your choice and joining a topical channel. You can download and install a number of different IRC chat programs enabling you to chat on IRC servers.

IRQ Each IRQ (interrupt request) line in a system connects a particular device with the CPU. The device uses the IRQ to signal the CPU when the device is ready to send or receive information. Each device on your system requires its own IRQ.

ISA The Industry Standard Architecture bus, one of the earliest types of an I/O bus. The EISA bus followed the ISA bus a few years later. (See also *bus* and *EISA*.)

ISDN This acronym stands for Integrated Services Digital Network. ISDN lines are high-capacity phone lines, often used to connect to the Internet, which can carry about 128Kbps. For you to use an ISDN connection, your phone company must install an ISDN line to your location. You connect using an ISDN modem. Your ISP must also provide ISDN service.

ISP (Internet Service Provider) A company that provides connections to the Internet, typically for a monthly fee. Individuals can connect to an ISP account via a Dial-Up Networking connection. Companies and other organizations can purchase other types of connections and services, as well, such as Web site hosting. (See *Dial-Up Networking*.)

 If you don't have an ISP, you can use the Internet Connection Wizard to find one. Or, you can check your yellow pages under "computers" or "Internet."

italic An attribute or style you apply to text to make it look *slanted*, or *italicized*. In many applications, you can press [Ctrl]+[I] to apply italics to selected text.

J

jack Generally, a receptacle into which you plug some type of connector. Most often, the term "jack" applies to phone line connections.

Java A programming language designed to create compact, portable programs easily transmitted online or on a network. Sun Microsystems developed Java and currently ships the programming language as the Java Development Kit.

Java applet Each small, individual Java application, or applet, performs a special function. Because of their small size and portability, Web page developers add Java applications to Web pages to enhance page capabilities. For example, a Web page developer can insert a Java applet that displays a stock ticker or flashing billboard, acts as an interactive catalog, or runs an interactive animation. (In contrast, JavaBean, or Bean, is a reusable Java component that a program can use to create an applet).

Java Virtual Machine The self-contained operating environment in which Java applets run. The Java Virtual Machine (VM) operates separately from the operating system. This means that Java applets can run on any system with a VM, whether it's a UNIX, Macintosh, or Windows-based system. The VM also provides security and reliability, since applet files don't affect any system files. Java-capable browsers, like the recent versions of Netscape Navigator and Internet Explorer, include a VM that enables the browser to run Java applets.

JavaScript An HTML subset that enables a Web page designer to incorporate Java features by typing commands into the Web page's HTML file.

Jaz drive A type of removable disk drive manufactured by Iomega Corp. The Jaz 1G uses 1G disk cartridges, while the Jaz 2G uses 2G cartridges (Figure J.1). Both internal and external Jaz models, connect via a SCSI connection, so you need a SCSI adapter on your system to use a Jaz. (See also *adapter* and *removable disk*.)

Figure J.1 A removable disk drive, like the Jaz 2G, enables you to increase the disk storage for your system to a nearly unlimited degree.

joystick A device with a movable handle that you use to move the mouse pointer or control other on-screen information. A joystick works better than a mouse or keyboard for many computer games.

.JPG (JPEG)   .JPG (Windows) or .JPEG (Mac) files are types of graphic files typically found on Web pages. An image in the .JPG format can be up to 96% smaller in file size than the same image in another graphic file format. While the .JPG format may not provide as much detail, it works well for graphics meant to be decorative rather than informative.

jumper A small connector between two pins on a circuit board that creates a connection between the pins. You change the jumper position to configure a setting on a circuit board, usually a motherboard or modem in a PC. (See also *DIP switch*.)

justify A type of alignment that inserts spacing between words and letters to expand each line of text to span between document margins or the sides of a cell.

> This text in this paragraph is **justified**. Justified text means that the text in both the left and right margins will line up evenly. The last line in a justified paragraph may not go all the way to the right margin.¶

Figure J.2 This is an example of justified text.

K

K A K represents 1,024 bytes of information, when referring to storing information. For example, 100K is 100 kilobytes. When referring to transmitting information, the K represents the decimal value, 1,000. (See also *Kbps*.)

 If you hear someone use "K" when describing a modem speed, as in "I have a 56K modem," the person doesn't mean kilobytes. He or she means "Kbps," a data transmission measure.

KB This abbreviation, like K, designates a measurement presented in kilobytes.

Kbps *Kbps* stands for *kilobits per second*, or 1,000 bits per second. A 56K modem generally can transfer about 56,000 bps, but some are capable of transferring data at 57,600 bps (with the extra transmission speed provided via data compression and other features).

 The FCC limits data transmission speeds over phone lines. Although some modems can work at 56K, the FCC limits data receiving speeds to 53K, so your modem generally won't connect at a speed greater than 53K on a regular phone line.

kerning Adjusting the spacing between letters to reduce the appearance of apparent gaps in words. For example, "i" and "l" need less spacing before and after the letters because they're narrow. Other letters, such as "k," require more spacing before or after to prevent them from blending into other characters. Many fonts have built-in kerning. Some word processors and page layout programs also enable you to manually kern letters.

key The keyboard is made up of keys that you press to enter information into the computer. A key may also be a special code or password you need to decrypt information. Finally, your database program may use the term "key" to refer to a criterion you enter when you want to search or query the database. (See also *decrypt/decryption*.)

keyboard The keyboard is made up of all the letter, number, and character keys that you use to enter information into the computer, as well as special keys that you can use to select commands.

93

You can buy split keyboards that help you hold your arms at more comfortable angles. There are also keyboards with built-in wrist rests to reduce the repetitive-motion injury called carpal-tunnel syndrome. If you buy a new keyboard, make sure it uses the same type of connection as your old one and that your system has the right type of port. For example, if you buy a USB keyboard, the system needs to have a USB port.

keyboard repeat rate A measurement of how quickly a character repeats on the screen if you press and hold a key. You can adjust the repeat rate to make the keyboard more or less sensitive. Choose Start| Settings|Control Panel, then double-click the Keyboard icon in the Control Panel window. Use the dialog box shown in Figure K.1 to change the settings.

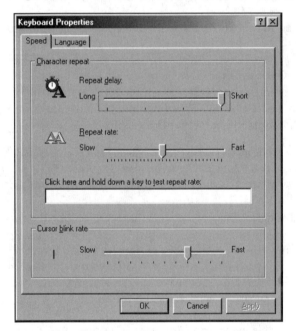

Figure K.1 You can adjust the keyboard repeat rate and other keyboard settings in this dialog box.

keypad The 10-key group of extra number keys and mathematical operators that appears on some keyboards. (See also *enhanced keyboard* and *numeric keypad*.)

keyword In AOL, you use a keyword to jump to a particular AOL service.

kiosk A kiosk is a stand in a public place that houses a computer providing a specific type of information or service. A kiosk at a trade show might display an interactive demonstration. A kiosk at a department store might dispense gift certificates, create a greeting card, or enable you to register for a gift service.

Knowledge Base (Microsoft) Microsoft Technical Support offers the Knowledge Base, an online, searchable listing of articles that cover a variety of "how to" and technical questions about Microsoft's products.

 Go to http://www.microsoft.com/support/ to search the Knowledge Base.

L

label Text that you enter in a spreadsheet cell to identify data below or beside it.

LAN (local area network) A Local Area Network connects a number of computers so that they share resources on a dedicated file server. A single LAN can serve a few computers or hundreds, but usually the LAN serves only one location or company. In contrast, the Internet is a much broader type of network. (See also *WAN*.)

landscape orientation A wide page format that turns the page so that the longer side runs along the top edge. Landscape orientation fits more information on each line or row of the document. (See also *portrait orientation*.)

Laplink The Laplink application connects your notebook (or another computer) to your desktop computer via modem, cable, or network. You can then use your notebook to control the desktop computer and run the applications from that desktop computer. You also can use Laplink to transfer and update files between computers, keeping all your information current.

laptop (see notebook computer)

laser pointer A pen-sized device that emits a beam of red light, which you can use to point to information on a projection screen or other large board during a presentation.

 Use caution with a laser pointer; don't shine it into any person's or animal's eyes, because it can cause permanent damage.

laser printer Laser printers print high-quality hard copies. Laser printers achieve high-print resolutions by using electrostatic reproduction. A fine laser charges areas on a photostatic drum or belt. As the drum or belt rotates, it applies the toner that was attracted to the charged areas to the page. A laser printer offers better print quality than an inkjet printer and also prints faster.

launch Another word for starting an application. For example, "Launch Microsoft Excel" means to start the Excel program.

LCD projector A type of projector to which you connect a PC to project information from the PC onto a large screen. LCD projectors usually include a remote control, allowing the presenter to control the presentation. (See also *DLP (Digital Light Processing) Projector*.)

left align Aligning information to the left margin, the left side of the cell, or the left side of the object holding it. Left alignment yields an uneven appearance at the right side of a block of text, called ragged right. (See also *alignment* and *flush left, flush right*.)

letter quality Letter quality printing means a high quality printing suitable for formal correspondence. Some printers can also print at a lower quality, both to speed up printing and reduce the amount of toner and other print materials used. (See also *draft*.)

link In OLE (Object Linking and Embedding), you can paste a linked copy of information from one document (the source document) into another (the target or destination document). When you update the original information, the linked copy updates as well, ensuring that the two files always contain identical information. In spreadsheet programs, you can create linking formulas to establish manual links between files. (See also *OLE*.)

LINUX An alternative UNIX-based operating system that's free and runs on many platforms, including PCs, Macintoshes, and Amigas. LINUX can be used for networking and as the operating system for an e-mail, Web page, or newsgroups server.

list box A list box in a dialog box lists a number of choices (Figure L.1). You typically can scroll to display additional choices, and then click the choice you want to apply.

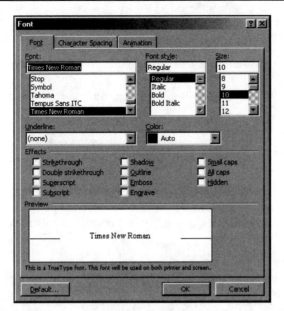

Figure L.1 List boxes, like the three at the top of this dialog box, present a list of choices.

load After you start a program, your computer loads the program into memory. That is, the system transfers the program instructions from the hard disk to RAM. Web browser software also loads a Web page when it receives the page information and displays it on the screen after you click a link or specify a Web address to display.

local bus A type of bus that skips the main data or I/O bus and instead directly connects an adapter with the CPU. The VESA Local Bus or VL-Bus came first for 486 systems. Pentium or better systems use the PCI local bus. Note that the local bus doesn't replace other system buses; it supplements them. (See also *bus, EISA, expansion bus,* and *ISA.*)

log in or log on These terms describe the process of providing information to connect to a LAN (local area network) or an Internet connection. For example, to connect with an ISP, your system needs to send your username and password to verify that you have an Internet account. Most communications software make the log on process automatic.

log off When your computer logs off a network connection, it sends information to the server or ISP computer to terminate the connection. Without a log off process, the server or ISP computer would leave the connection open, potentially preventing other computers from connecting.

LOL This abbreviation of the phrase "laughing out loud" can be used in response to a joke in an e-mail message or newsgroup posting.

Lotus 1-2-3 The spreadsheet program (Figure L.2) published by Lotus Development Corp. 1-2-3 was the first major spreadsheet on the market, taking advantage of the PC's ability to perform calculations rapidly and accurately.

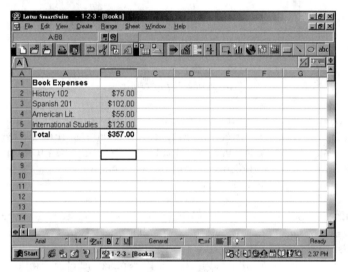

Figure L.2 A Lotus 1-2-3 spreadsheet

lowercase Text presented in all small letters.

LPT port Another name for a parallel port, a type of port to which you usually connect a printer or external removable disk drive. "LPT" was the name DOS used for a parallel port. Most systems have a single parallel port called LPT1. When you set up your printer under Windows, you designate that you've connected it to LPT1. (See also *port* and *printer port*.)

 Parallel ports are inexpensive, easy to add to your system, and save you the trouble of plugging in and unplugging printers and other devices.

LS-120 disk Although this type of removable disk looks just like a 3 ½-inch floppy disk, an LS-120 disk holds up to 120M of information. The LS-120 drive can also read from and write to 1.44M floppy disks, making the LS-120 a convenient choice for a new system or a convenient upgrade for an older system. The LS-120 drive uses floptical technology. (See also *3 ½-inch disk* and *floptical*.)

lurk You can lurk in an Internet newsgroup. When you lurk, you read messages posted by others but don't post messages yourself.

M

M or MB These abbreviations stand for megabyte, a disk storage measurement. Each megabyte is 1,048,576 bytes of data. You also may see MB used to describe data throughput (data transfer) speed, in which case it stands for 1,000,000 bytes. Each M holds 1,024 K, equaling 1,024 x 1,024 bytes or characters of information. (See also *K*.)

Macintosh In 1984, Apple introduced the Macintosh (or Mac), one of the earliest personal computers. The graphical user interface and mouse quickly made the Mac popular. The current Mac model, called Power Macintosh systems, offers one of the fastest CPUs on the market. While the Mac operating system isn't compatible with Windows, you can use a variety of utilities to convert and transfer files between a Mac and a Windows-based PC.

macro Creating a macro in a program is essentially creating your own custom command. In many applications, you can record a series of commands and save them as a macro. Then, when you run the macro, the application performs the steps that you recorded. Some applications also offer a macro programming language so that you can create more complex macros.

mail merge The mail merge feature in a word processing program is used to create a mass mailing, including envelopes and mailing labels. The mail merge inserts information from a database into specified locations (fields) in the word processor document, creating one personalized copy of a letter for each record in the database. For example, the mail merge reads each record in a database, then inserts a recipient's name and address at the top of a copy of the letter, and the recipient's first name in the greeting line. (See also *database*, *field*, and *record*.)

mail server The computer and/or software that routes and stores e-mail messages on a LAN or on the Internet. If you connect to the Internet via an ISP, the ISP's mail server sends outgoing e-mail messages and receives and stores incoming messages until you connect and retrieve them with your e-mail program.

mailbox Every user on a mail server has a designated storage area called a mailbox. Until the user retrieves his or her messages via e-mail, the mailbox holds them.

male connector A receptacle on a device, or on one end of a cable, that has pins. The pins plug into the pinholes on a matching female connector. (See also *female connector*.)

MAPI MAPI, the Messaging Application Program Interface, enables applications, like your word processor and spreadsheet, to communicate with your e-mail program. For example, with MAPI, you can choose File|Send To|Mail Recipient to create a new e-mail message with the open document file inserted as an attachment.

 Some e-mail programs handle MAPI messages by default. In other e-mail programs, you may have to choose an option to enable your e-mail program as the "MAPI client," meaning that it can handle MAPI messages.

manual page break (see hard page break)

margin The white space at the edge of the page around the contents of a printout forms the margin. A page with narrower margins can hold more information.

Some printers limit the size of the margins you can use in a document. For example, some printers can't print within .25" of the edges of the page and will "cut off" information falling in the unprintable area.

master/slave (or host/slave) When you connect certain kinds of devices, you create a master/slave relationship in which the master device can control the slave device. For example, if you connect more than one hard disk drive to a single IDE drive connector within the system, the first hard disk becomes the master and the second becomes the slave. The master disk starts up first and recognizes the slave disk after receiving a special signal.

math coprocessor Also called a numeric coprocessor, a math coprocessor handles high level mathematical computations. The coprocessor can perform the calculations 10 to 100 times faster than the CPU itself can. Some 486 CPUs, like the Intel 486DX, include a built-in math coprocessor, as do Pentium and Pentium II CPUs. (See also *coprocessor*.)

104

maximize To return a file or application window to its full size. A maximized application window fills the Windows desktop. A maximized file window fills the working area within the application window.

Maximize button One of three buttons at the right end of the title bar in a file window or application window. You can click the Maximize button to maximize the window. After the window is maximized, the Maximize button changes to the Restore button. (See also *Restore button*.)

McAfee VirusScan Network Associates publishes McAfee VirusScan, one of the leading virus scanning utility programs available. Virus scanning software checks your computer's files for known computer viruses and removes those viruses. McAfee also can scan files as you download or copy them to your system and alert you to infected files. (See also *virus*.)

Many new systems come installed with McAfee VirusScan or another virus checker. You can download a demo version of McAfee VirusScan from *http://www.mcafee.com*.

media The different types of disks used to store information, such as hard disks, floppy disks, removable disks, and CD-RWs are referral to as media. The term media also applies to different types of multimedia files, such as sound and video files.

Media Player This Windows applet (Figure M.1) plays different types of multimedia files including MPEG video, .AVI (Video for Windows), MIDI sound files, .WAV sound files, and CD Audio. To start the Media Player, choose Start|Programs|Accessories|Multimedia|Media Player (Windows 95) or Start|Programs|Accessories|Entertainment|Media Player (Windows 98).

Figure M.1 The Media Player can play .AVI and .MPEG video files, among other types.

memory The term memory describes any chip in a PC that holds the values and instructions the system needs to run. A ROM (Read-Only Memory) chip holds a set of permanent instructions the system needs to start up. RAM (Random-Access Memory) serves as the working memory for your computer. RAM holds program instructions or information that you've entered into a file but haven't yet saved. Information moves through RAM as you perform different tasks with the PC. Shutting down the computer clears everything out of RAM. Most PCs come with at least 32M of RAM. VRAM (Video Random-Access Memory) chips on the system's video card help transfer information between the CPU and the video card to speed up the video display.

 Remember, when you save a file, the computer doesn't save it to memory. Instead, the computer stores it on a disk. Disks store files, and memory holds working information.

memory cache A cache that holds data the CPU needs frequently, reducing the time it takes for the CPU to retrieve data that it would normally have to find in the RAM. Traditionally, a cache within the CPU is called an internal cache or Level 1 (L1) cache, while a cache on the motherboard is called an external cache, or Level 2 (L2) cache. However, the Pentium II processor includes both L1 and L2 caches. In theory, a larger cache size (512K versus 256K, for example) can improve system performance.

Computer & Internet Dictionary

memory card (see flash memory card)

menu A menu lists commands in a program. Each menu groups commands for similar tasks. For example, the File menu lists commands for working with files and the Format menu lists commands for formatting either selected information or the whole file. To open a menu, click the menu name. Then you can choose a command listed in the menu.

menu bar The menu bar lists each of the menus in an application and usually appears near the top of the application window under the window title bar. To open a menu, click its name on the menu bar. To close a menu, click outside it or press [Esc] twice (to both close the menu and deselect the menu name).

message box A message box looks like a dialog box but appears for informational reasons only (rather than enabling you to choose command options, as does a dialog box). An application displays a message box to inform you when it has finished a particular operation, such as a spell check. Click OK to acknowledge and close the message box. (See also *dialog box*.)

MHz When measuring the frequency of a device that operates in waves or cycles (such as electrical vibrations), one hertz equals one cycle per second. Thus, one megahertz (MHz) equals 1,000,000 cycles per second.

microprocessor An integrated circuit chip capable of accepting and executing instructions. The microprocessor (CPU) controls most of a PC's operations. (See also *central processing unit*.)

Microsoft Microsoft publishes many of the leading application programs used on PCs today, as well as the Windows and Windows NT operating systems. Microsoft's other products include Office (Word, Excel, PowerPoint, Access, and Outlook), FrontPage, Works, Encarta, Golf, Publisher, and a number of other applications.

Microsoft Network The Microsoft Network serves as both an ISP and a Web site (Figure M.2). Like other ISP home pages, the home page for the Microsoft Network (MSN) enables you to follow links to information about topics of interest, like information about your favorite stocks. If you access the Internet through MSN, your e-mail address end with msn.com.

107

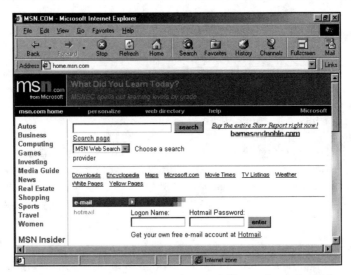

Figure M.2 You can visit the Microsoft Network on the Web.

MIDI The MIDI (Musical Instrument Digital Interface) standard defines how musical devices, like electronic keyboards, can connect to and exchange information with a PC. Computers store MIDI music as MIDI (.MID) files, and a variety of sequencer programs allow users to play and edit MIDI files. For example, Media Players in Windows plays MIDI files.

millennium bug (see Y2K)

MIME The MIME (Multipurpose Internet Mail Extensions) format is used for encoding and transferring Internet e-mail. Many e-mail programs automatically encode with MIME or decode MIME files. (See also *decode* and *encode*.)

minimize To reduce a file or application window to its smallest size. A minimized application window becomes a button on the Windows taskbar. A minimized file window reduces to an icon or bar in the application window's working area.

Minimize button One of three buttons at the right end of the title bar for a file or application window. The Minimize button has a small bar or underline on it. You can click the Minimize button to minimize the window. After you minimize the window, click the taskbar button or icon for the minimized window to restore it. (See also *restore*.)

Computer & Internet Dictionary

minitower A minitower is a style of case for a PC's system unit, the body of the computer into which you plug the keyboard, monitor, and other devices. The minitower case stands on end to conserve desk space (unlike a desktop case, which sits horizontally) and is slightly smaller than a full-sized tower case.

MIPS MIPS (Million Instructions Per Second) measurements compare how rapidly a CPU processes program instructions. The higher the MIPS value, the better the system performed.

If you're looking for a new PC, try computing magazines like *PC/Computing* or *PC Magazine*, either at the newsstand or at their Web sites. Computing magazines routinely run benchmark tests to compare how various systems perform.

MIS Short for Management Information Systems, the business discipline that focuses on using Information Technology (computers and networking) to automate a business and make it more efficient.

MMX Intel created MMX, a set of 57 extra instructions and other features for handling multimedia tasks, to enhance its Pentium chips. Most systems sold today use MMX-enabled CPUs.

modem A modem (an abbreviation of MOdulator-DEModulator) converts digital computer information into an analog format and sends it over phone lines. A modem also converts analog information it receives back into a digital format that a computer can display and store. A PC must have a modem to connect with the Internet or any online service.

monitor The TV-like unit that displays computer information. The video card or display card in the PC draws screen images and then sends them to the monitor for display. Monitors come in different sizes and with other capabilities that determine the quality of the monitor image. For example, a monitor can display at different resolutions like (640x480, 800x600, and 1024x768). Dot pitch measures how close the beams of light are on the monitor face; a lower dot pitch measurement produces a better picture. Color depth describes how many colors a monitor can display; many today display up to 16.8 million colors.

If the monitor doesn't support all the same features that the video card does, the monitor may not work with the video card. So, don't buy a new monitor without making sure your video card can take advantage of all its capabilities.

109

motherboard This circuit board holds the essential components of the PC, including the CPU, ROM, RAM, buses, and slots for adapters. The brand and model of motherboard determine what features it includes. For example, some motherboards today feature built-in (on board) networking or video. You can substantially upgrade a PC by replacing its motherboard, CPU, and RAM.

mouse A device that you roll on your desk to move a pointer on the screen. You use the pointer and the buttons on the mouse to select commands, text, and objects on the screen, or even to draw. Because you use the mouse to give the computer information, it's also called an input device. (See also *trackball*.)

mouse button A pressable mechanism on the mouse that you use to perform a computer action based on the on-screen mouse pointer location. A typical Windows-based system uses a two-button mouse. To click with the mouse, move the mouse pointer over an item on the screen and press and release the left mouse button once. To double-click, position the pointer and quickly press and release the left mouse button twice.

mouse pad A portable rubberized pad on which you move the mouse. The ball within the mouse has better traction on a mouse pad than on a slick desk surface, so a mouse pad allows the mouse to operate more smoothly.

> Remember to clean your mouse pad occasionally. A lot of dirt can build up on the mouse ball, causing the mouse to work erratically. The bottom of the mouse has a cover that you can remove to clean the mouse. Remove the cover and ball, blow out any dust, use a slightly wet cotton swab to clean the inside, and replace the ball and cover.

move In an application, to remove a selection from its current location and place it in another location. When both original and final locations appear on the same page or screen, you often can drag the selection into place. In other cases, you need to use the Edit|Cut command to remove the information from its original location and then use the Edit|Paste command to paste the information into the new location. (See also *Clipboard*.)

MPEG .MPEG or .MPG files are a special type of audio or video file compressed via the MPEG (Moving Pictures Experts Group) standard. Because MPEG files can pack a lot of video information into a relatively small file size, you may encounter MPEG files while browsing the Web. You can either play or download MPEG files from a Web site.

MS-DOS Also called simply DOS, the Microsoft Disk Operating System (MS-DOS) was introduced for personal computers in 1981. MS-DOS controlled basic system operation and let the user give commands to the system. MS-DOS is a command-line operating system that allows you to enter commands at a command prompt.

multimedia Applications or presentations that integrate text, graphics, audio, video, and (often) interactive features. For example, CD-ROM encyclopedias display text on the screen, but you also can play sounds, view photos and maps, play video clips, and move easily between encyclopedia entries.

multitasking This is when a computer executes commands from more than one program at a time. For example, if you use your Web browser to start downloading a large file from the Internet and then switch to your word processor to format text while the file downloads, your computer is multitasking. (See also *background*.)

My Computer A Windows 95 or 98 window that contains an icon for each of your disk drives, as well as icons for the Control Panel and Printers, which you use to work with the devices attached to your system. It may also include the Dial-Up Networking and Scheduled Tasks icons. You can double-click the icon for a disk drive to use the My Computer window to work with the folders and files on a disk.

Double-click to open My Computer.

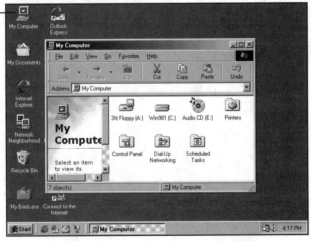

Figure M.3 Open the My Computer window to see your disk drives and other key features.

My Documents Windows (or an Office application you install) creates the \My Documents\ folder and uses it as a default location for storing and opening files. Windows 98 even includes a My Documents icon on the desktop. You can double-click that icon to see what the My Documents folder holds.

N

navigate To move around in a file or on the Web. In an application, navigation entails displaying another page, moving the insertion point, or selecting another cell. On the Web, navigating means moving from page to page on a Web site or displaying another site altogether.

netBIOS The netBIOS (Network Basic Input/Output System) enables an individual PC to connect to a LAN and work with the network's devices. The netBIOS loads with the rest of the network operating system on the individual PC. (See also *LAN*.)

Netcaster This feature in Netscape Communicator enables you to connect to channels (much like subscribing to a channel in Internet Explorer 4.0). You use Netcaster to select Web pages (channels) and choose how often the Web sites should update them. When scheduled, your system will download the channel content from the Web sites automatically. Then, you can browse the downloaded pages when you have time. (See also *Netscape Communicator* and *push content*.)

netiquette A set of rules for behaving on the Internet. Netiquette helps Internet users treat each other with courtesy and use the Net's resources wisely. Here are a few netiquette rules:

1. Never type in ALL CAPS. It's the equivalent of screaming.
2. To emphasize a word, enclose it between *asterisks.*
3. When posting a newsgroup reply, snip out all but the relevant text to keep the message short.
4. Don't send spam.
5. Don't pick on newbies. Politely direct them to resources or help.

(See also *flame, newbie,* and *spam*.)

Netscape Communicator This suite of Internet programs published by Netscape Communications Corp. includes the Navigator Web browser, as well as e-mail, newsgroup reader, Web page design, and Internet conferencing software.

113

Netscape Navigator   The Web browser published by Netscape Communications Corp. (See Figure N.1.) You can go to *http://home.netscape.com* to download Navigator and other Netscape products.

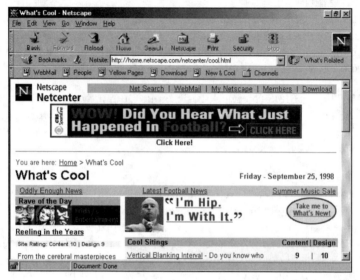

Figure N.1 The Netscape Navigator browser.

Netware   LAN network operating system (NOS) software published by Novell. The NOS software controls the flow of information over the network.

network   A group of connected computers that can exchange information. Computers connected to the network may also share central devices, such a file storage, a fast modem or Internet connection, or a printer. Generally, the networked computers are connected via cabling, and network operating software controls the network operation. However, with Dial-Up Networking or another type of communications software, remote users also can connect to a network by modem.

network adapter   The network adapter card (also called a NIC or network interface card) installs in a PC so that you can connect the PC to a network. Connect one end of the cabling to the network adapter card and the other to a network connection such as a hub. (The type of network connection depends on the network layout and type of cabling.)

Computer & Internet Dictionary

Network Neighborhood If your Windows-based system is connected to a network, you can double-click the Network Neighborhood icon to open the Network Neighborhood window. It identifies all the shared resources on the network that your computer can access, such as shared disk drives and printers.

newbie A newbie is an inexperienced computer user, particularly someone new at working online.

newsgroup More formally called USENET newsgroups, these are electronic message boards where users can post a question or article or reply to an existing post. Each newsgroup covers a particular topic, so you may choose to join and view those newsgroups that interest you. (See also *post* and *thread*.)

newsgroup server A computer or software that routes and stores newsgroup messages on the Internet. If you connect to the Internet via an ISP, the ISP usually offers a newsgroup server as well.

newsreader Any software that you use to read and post newsgroup messages. You may install a special newsreader like Internet mail, or use another program like Outlook Express (Figure N.2), which offers newsreading capabilities along with e-mail and other features.

N

115

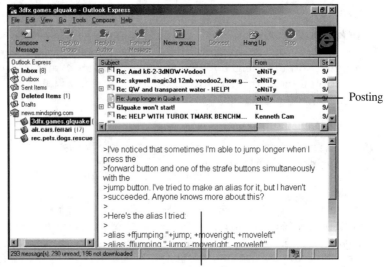

Figure N.2 Outlook Express, which comes with Window 98 and IE4, lets you connect to and read newsgroups.

NNTP NNTP (Network News Transport Protocol) is the communications method used by news servers and newsreaders to send messages over the Internet.

node Any individual PC or workstation connected to a LAN. The term node also may refer to other devices connected to the LAN.

Norton Utilities A popular utility program offering a variety of features for maintaining disk information and repairing damaged disks, as well as fixing Windows and application programs.

notebook computer These portable, compact size computers, also called laptops, transport easily and open like a notebook for use. A notebook weighs about 5-9 pounds. While older notebooks performed substantially worse, dollar for dollar, than desktop systems, the price and performance gap between current notebooks and desktops has narrowed substantially. (See also *desktop computer*.)

Notepad With this Windows applet, you can create plain text (.TXT) documents that are easy to exchange between applications. Most applications can open or import .TXT files. To start Notepad in Windows 95 or 98, choose Start|Programs|Accessories|Notepad.

Novell The Utah-based company that developed the Netware networking operating system (NOS) software, the leading networking software for several years.

null In programming, a null set is empty and has no value. In contrast, 0 represents the value 0.

null modem cable You can use a null modem cable to connect two computers to transfer information without using a modem or networking connection. However, you may need special software to make the connection. (See also *Direct Cable Connection*.)

number format In a spreadsheet program, applying a number format to selected cells controls how numbers appear in those cells. For example, if you apply a percent number format, the numbers display as percentages, including the % sign. Choosing a currency format adds a dollar sign and two decimal places.

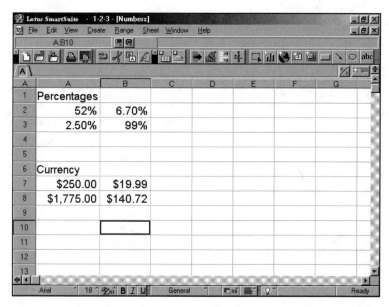

*Figure N.3 The upper numbers here use a percent format.
The lower ones use a currency format.*

numbered list In a word processor document, you can number each item in a list, as in a list of ordered steps. Top word processors can number a list automatically for you. Click the numbering button to turn on the numbering feature, type, and press [Enter] after each list item.

NumLock key On an enhanced keyboard, you press ⟨Num Lock⟩ to toggle the numeric keypad at the far right side between typing numbers and working as arrow (insertion point movement) keys. (See also *enhanced keyboard*.)

numeric keypad Another name for the 10-key keypad to the right of the main group of keyboard keys on an enhanced keyboard.

O

object This term describes any non-text item you insert into a file. For example, a piece of clip art or other graphic is an object that you can select, format, and move. When referring to OLE, an object also refers to a section of another file that you've pasted or embedded into the container document. (See also *OLE*.)

object-oriented programming In object-oriented programming, the programmer can save instructions performing a particular function as a single module. Then, when building a full program, the programmer can insert previously created modules rather than writing out complete instructions. The programmer can insert a module into any program requiring the module's function. Object-oriented programming saves programming and typing time.

OCR OCR (Optical Character Recognition) software works with a scanner. When the scanner scans a page of text or numbers, the OCR software converts the text or numbers to characters, which can then transfer the information to a word processor or other program. This allows you to edit or format the information.

.OCX A file name extension that identifies a custom control used in Visual Basic programming. A programmer can insert an .OCX control in a programming project and set properties to define the control's function. The programmer distributes the original .OCX file along with the finished program's .EXE file and other files for the program. .OCX files will appear on your computer's hard disk. .OCX controls work with OLE. (See also *.VBX*.)

The controls used in object-oriented programming save a tremendous amount of programming time. Rather than creating common program elements like dialog box list boxes repeatedly, the programmer can simply insert the list box control and set properties (options) for it. Custom controls come in .OCX and .VBX files.

ODBC ODBC stands for Open Database Connectivity, a method databases and other programs use to exchange data stored in a database format. For certain data features to work in applications, your system must have ODBC drivers (files that provide the ODBC capability) installed. Applications that require ODBC drivers typically install the drivers automatically.

OEM Original Equipment Manufacturers (OEMs) manufacture hardware components. Secondary companies assemble the components into a finished piece of hardware, such as a full PC.

Office Office, from Microsoft, is the best-selling software suite. The standard edition of office includes Word (word processor), Excel (spreadsheet), PowerPoint (presentation graphics), and Outlook (e-mail and scheduling). The professional edition adds Access (database).

offline When a printer is offline it is not ready to receive data. Also, when not connected to the Internet or another online service, your system is offline. In Windows 98, you can download information from the Web or a newsgroup, and then read that information while offline to reduce connect time.

> If your printer is offline, look for the Online or Ready button, and press it to put the printer online.

OK button Most dialog boxes include an OK button. Click the OK button to apply your choices and close the dialog box.

OLE OLE (Object Linking and Embedding) technology enables applications to share information and tools. You can copy an object or information from one application (the source application), and insert it as a linked object in the destination (or target) application. Whenever you make changes to the original information in the source document, the destination document changes to match. You also can embed an OLE object without copying it from another location. To do so, use the Insert|Object command and select the type of object to insert. The tools for creating that type of object appear. For example, if you insert an Excel object in Word, Excel's tools appear so that you can create the spreadsheet information. Double-click an embedded object to change it.

online A printer is online when it's ready to receive data; an indicator light on the top of the printer usually lights up when the printer is online and ready. Also, when connected to the Internet or another online service, your system is online.

online community Online community can refer to a specific online service like AOL or CompuServe, or it can refer to a BBS, any online meeting place. It also refers to particular Web sites that serve as entry points or gathering places on the Internet. For example, *http://www.excite.com* has evolved from a search engine to a site offering news, classifieds, shopping, and more to provide users with a central entry point for a variety of services.

opaque When you apply a fill to a graphic object, an opaque fill obscures anything behind the object. That is, you can't see through an opaque object. (See also *transparent*.)

open To start or launch an application. When you're working with a program, you open a file to load it into RAM, display it on the screen, and begin working. In most applications, you can use the File|Open command to open files.

operating system The operating system is the software that runs the internal components of the computer, such as MS-DOS, Windows, or the Macintosh operating system (MacOS). The operating system software directs information from the keyboard into the system; between the CPU, RAM, and other system components; and from the system to devices like the monitor and the printer. Applications run "on top" of the operating system.

operators In a spreadsheet program, operators are the mathematical symbols in a formula that specify how the formula should calculate. For example, you can use the + (addition), * (multiplication), / (division), and < (less than) operators, among others. You also may use operators when you query a database to make the query more precise.

optical disk Any disk that has reflective pits read by a laser. CD-ROM and DVD-ROM discs both are optical disk formats. A magneto optical (MO) disk and disk drive work slightly differently. In this format, a laser heats a location on the disk so that a read/write head can change the magnetic orientation in a spot to write information to it. MO disks come in both 3 ½-inch and 5 ¼-inch formats. Some users might use the general term optical disk to refer to magneto optical disks, as well.

option button Option buttons appear in groups in dialog boxes (Figure O.1). Option buttons present mutually exclusive options. That is, you can click only one of the option buttons at a time. Option buttons used to be called *radio buttons*, a name you may still encounter occasionally.

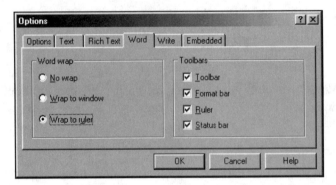

Figure O.1 Option buttons appear in groups, like those at the left side of this dialog box.

options Choices offered in a dialog box or list.

Organizer Lotus Organizer (Figure O.2) is the leading PIM (personal information manager) software. It's easy to use and looks like a paper date book. In addition to scheduling, Organizer offers an address book, call logging, a to do list, long term planning, note logging, and anniversary list features. (See also *PIM*.)

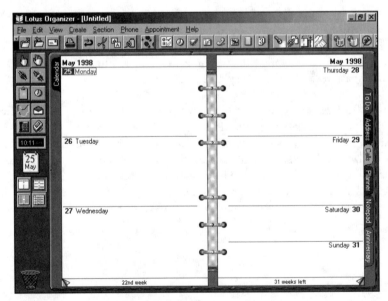

Figure O.2 Organizer looks like a date book, but offers many more features.

orphan When the first line of a paragraph appears as the last line on a page, that line is an orphan. You can correct an orphan by inserting a hard page break before it. In some word processors, you also can activate an option that prevents orphans by moving page breaks for you. (See also *widow*.)

outline feature Leading word processing, spreadsheet, and presentation graphics programs usually offer an outline feature. In a word processor or presentation graphics program, you can use the outline feature to enter and organize text before formatting it or to rearrange topics more quickly than you could in the normal view. In a spreadsheet, the outline feature groups values for subtotaling.

outbox The folder in your e-mail program where the e-mail program places messages to be sent. If you create messages while offline, the outbox holds the messages until you connect and send them. (See also *offline*.)

Outlook and Outlook Express Microsoft publishes these information management programs. Outlook comes as part of the Office suite (or can be purchased separately), and includes e-mail, scheduling, an address book, a to-do list, and journal features. Outlook serves as an enhanced PIM. Outlook Express comes with Windows 98 or Internet Explorer 4. Outlook Express focuses more on online features, offering e-mail, an address book, and newsreader capabilities. (See also *newsreader* and *PIM*.)

overtype mode In a word processing program, overtype mode will type over any text to the right of the insertion point. Each character or space you type replaces an existing character or space. Press [Insert] to switch between insert and overtype modes. (See also *insert mode*.)

P

packet Information transmitted on a network or the Internet is divided into blocks called packets. Each packet includes the data itself plus the destination information and error-checking information.

page Each printed sheet of information from an application equals a page. RAM also switches information in sections called pages.

page break A page break in an application is a mark showing where one page ends and the next begins in a printout. Word processors, presentation graphics, and page layout programs show page breaks on the screen automatically. In a database, you have to create a report to identify a page of information. Also, you have to insert page breaks manually or preview the printout to see them.

Page Down key Press [PgDn] on the keyboard to display the next screen of information, that is, the screen below the currently displayed area of the file.

page layout The page layout consists of any settings you make in a file to control the appearance of the printout pages. Settings such as the margins, orientation, and page size affect the page layout. (See also *footer*, *header*, *margin*, and *orientation*.)

 In many applications, you choose File | Page Setup to access the page setup settings.

page layout software Page layout programs perform desktop publishing, combining text and graphics and other page elements to form publications like newsletters and brochures. PageMaker (originally for the Macintosh) was one of the earliest and best page layout programs. Now, it competes with QuarkXPress, as well as other programs like Microsoft Publisher. Many current versions of word processing programs also offer page layout features, including the ability to format text in multiple columns. (See also *desktop publishing*.)

page numbering A feature that tells a program to print a page number on each page of a printout. You usually can insert the page number in the header or footer, but many word processors enable you to insert page numbers in any area of the document.

Page Up key Press [PgUp] on the keyboard to display the previous screen of information, the section of information above the currently displayed area of the file.

PageMaker A page layout (desktop publishing) program published by Adobe for the Macintosh and Windows. PageMaker offers excellent indexing, as well as precise formatting controls and styles for design consistency. Designers can convert PageMaker files directly to HTML (Web page) format.

PageMill This Adobe software allows users to design Web pages, organize the pages into a Web site, and publish the site to a Web server, where other users can view them.

paint program A paint program is used to create and edit bitmap graphics. Although you can drag to draw objects like rectangles in a paint program, you have to change individual pixels or dots to edit the image. Windows Paint is a paint program. (See also *bitmap graphic*.)

Paint Shop Pro This paint program from Jasc software has emerged as a popular and inexpensive alternative to professional programs. Paint Shop Pro offers a number of custom brushes and color effects. It enables you to import and save images in a variety of formats and even to create animated images for Web pages.

palette A palette (Figure P.1) presents color or pattern choices you can apply to selected text or objects in an application. Click the square for the color or pattern you want to apply to the selection.

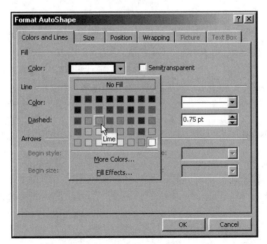

Figure P.1 Select a color to apply to an object or text by clicking the color.

pane In some applications, you can split a window into multiple areas called panes. Each pane shows a different part of the file or shows the file information using a different view. For example, a word processor might show a document outline in one pane and the normal document view in another pane. The current versions of the leading Web browsers also support Web page panes.

parallel cable A parallel cable will connect a device like a printer or a removable disk drive to the parallel (LPT) port on your system. The parallel cable typically has a 25-pin connector on one end and a Centronics connector (a long bar that plugs into a slot) on the other.

parallel port (see LPT port)

parameter You include a parameter with a DOS command or in a programming statement to specify how the computer should perform a particular operation. Some commands require parameters. Others don't and will use a default value if you don't enter a parameter.

parity Communicating computers sometimes use parity to check for errors. For each character (byte) transmitted, the sending computer sends an extra bit to identify whether the transmitted byte contained an even or odd number of binary 1s in the character. If the receiving computer finds that the extra bit and the number of 1s transmitted agree, it accepts the byte as valid. (See also *binary* and *bit*.)

parity bit During parity transmission, the extra bit used to verify parity is called the parity bit.

partition You can divide a hard disk into sections, called partitions, so that the system recognizes it as multiple disks. These aren't real physical disks, but are sections on the disk. You can install separate operating system software on each partition on the hard disk.

 You can use DOS to partition a hard disk or a utility program like Partition Magic, available at your local computer store, in computer catalogs, or online.

passive matrix A type of notebook display that uses transistors to pulse information to the liquid crystal cells that display colors. Passive matrix displays don't display as brightly as the currently standard active matrix displays, which provide a continuous charge to each cell and yield brighter color. (See also *active matrix*.)

password A secret code that you assign to a file, program, or Windows for security reasons. You must enter the password to open the file, program, or Windows. Users without the proper password cannot use your system or files.

paste When you copy or cut information, Windows places the information on the Clipboard. You can then insert that information into another location by pasting it from the Clipboard. To paste the information, move the insertion point to the desired location, then choose Edit|Paste or the Paste button. (See also *Clipboard*.)

path Also called the path name, the path identifies the precise location of a file on a disk. The path includes the disk letter (as in *C:*), the folder, any subfolders leading to the file with backslashes separating them (as in *My Documents\Memos*), and the file name and extension (*Memo.doc*). The full path to a file might look like *C:\My Documents\Memos\Memo.doc*. (See also *subfolder*.)

PC (personal computer) A complete computer system that can be used either as a stand-alone system or connected to a network. The initial PCs introduced in the early 80s were the first machines not to require a connection to a network or some type of larger, mainframe computer. They also were small enough to work in the more personal settings of a small office or home office. A PC includes all the key computer components, including the CPU, operating system, monitor, hard and floppy disk drives, input devices (mouse and keyboard), and a printer. Currently, PCs often come equipped with a modem and sound card and frequently include extra devices like a video camera.

PC Card Formerly called PCMCIA cards, these credit-card sized devices (Figure P.2) slide into slots on the side of a notebook computer. PC cards enable you to add a device or another item to the notebook without opening the notebook case. For example, you can add a PC Card modem or PC Card RAM to a notebook. Most newer notebooks can accept two Type II (5mm thick) or one Type III (10.5mm thick) PC Cards.

Figure P.2 Insert a PC Card in a notebook computer to add a feature such as a modem.

PC98 Standard Intel Corp., Microsoft Corp., and Compaq Computer Corp. jointly defined this set of standards for desktop PC hardware. PCs must comply with the standard to display the Windows logo. The standard requires faster buses, including either a 66MHz or 100MHz internal bus and a 64-bit PCI or AGP (accelerated graphics port) bus, among other requirements. (See also *bus*.)

PCI (see local bus)

PCMCIA (see PC card)

.PCX This file name extension identifies a type of bitmap file. You can create .PCX files with Paint Shop Pro or other paint programs. (See also *bitmap graphic* and *paint program*.)

PDA This acronym stands for Personal Digital Assistant, a handheld PC. (See also *hand-held PC*.)

.PDF The file name extension for Adobe Acrobat files, often found on the Web. Many types of files convert to the Acrobat format for reading and viewing with the Acrobat reader.

peer-to-peer network Each of the computers on a peer-to-peer network can access shared files on all other shared computers. Peer-to-peer networks work well in small office environments and don't require a designated file server. (See also *dedicated file server*.)

pen computing Using a computer with a special screen and software that recognizes printed words or writing on the screen with a stylus (pen).

Pentium This CPU from Intel supplanted 486 processors. The Pentium offered greater speed by supporting a 64-bit data bus. It also included a math co-processor and level 1 cache. The Pentium uses a Socket 7 connection on the motherboard. (See also *memory cache*.)

Pentium II The Pentium II CPU (Figure P.3) is the latest and fastest CPU from Intel. Available in speeds of 400MHz or more, the Pentium II includes built-in MMX support and plugs into the new Socket One slot. Faster Pentium IIs also take advantage of the 440BX 100 MHz chipset, significantly improving system speed.

Figure P.3 The Pentium II CPU powers many PCs today.

peripheral Peripherals are CPU-controlled devices connected to a PC, such as the display (video card and monitor), printer, and disk drives.

PERT chart This special chart offered in project management software plots out each task as a box, including the task start and end date and the length of time it requires. The chart uses arrows to indicate when you must finish one task before beginning the next. (See also *Project*.)

picture (see graphics)

PIF Under Windows 3.1, you create a .PIF (Program Information File) to give Windows the settings for running a DOS-based application. In Windows 95 and 98, you right-click the icon for the DOS/.EXE file in a My Computer or Windows Explorer window, and then change the settings as needed in the Properties dialog box.

PIM A PIM, or personal information manager, is a type of software that you can use to manage your schedule and contact list. Enter your appointments into the PIM software, and set it up to display a reminder prior to each appointment.

ping After your computer dials your Internet connection, you can "ping" the Internet Service Provider (ISP) computer to verify that the TCP/IP connection is working. When you send a ping via a TCP/IP connection, your system sends a signal to the ISP's system, which sends a response verifying that the connection is working properly.

> Windows includes the ping.exe utility (in the \Windows\ folder), which you can use to ping your ISP. Connect to your ISP, then choose Start | Programs | MS-DOS Prompt to open a DOS window. Type *cd \windows* and press Enter to display the C:\WINDOWS> prompt, if needed. Type *ping*, press space, and type the IP address for your ISP, including the periods. Press Enter, and the ISP computer should send a response.

Computer & Internet Dictionary

PhotoShop This paint program from Adobe enables you to create and work with bitmap images. PhotoShop offers professional features for retouching scanned photos and adding special-effects filters.

Photo CD The Photo CD (.PCD) format, developed by Kodak, stores digital images on CD-ROM. Some film processors will not only develop your 35mm film but also convert each image to digital .PCD format and store it on a CD.

pixel (pronounced picks-ell) An abbreviation for PICture Element, pixel refers to a dot comprising a graphic image. Your monitor displays everything in small dots of color, or pixels. Bitmap graphics also are formed in pixels. When you edit a bitmap graphic, you change the color for individual pixels.

Plug and Play Windows 95 introduced this specification for installing new hardware. When you add a new hardware component and start your system, Windows recognizes the new device and either installs the driver files (software that runs the device) automatically or asks you for the disk holding the driver files. Windows also automatically ensures that the plug and play device doesn't try to use system resources already in use by another device.

plug-in Plug-in programs help your Web browser software do something it can't do on its own. For example, the browser may need a plug-in program to play a certain type of video file. Some plug-ins download and install automatically when you need them. In other instances, you will need to download and install the plug-in manually. Some other programs, like certain graphics programs, also work with plug-ins that add features.

point To move the mouse pointer over an object on the screen. For example, if an instruction tells you to "Point to the Start button," you should move the mouse until the mouse pointer rests over the Start button on the taskbar.

pointer The on-screen symbol that moves when you move your mouse.

pointer speed The pointer speed refers to how far and fast the mouse pointer moves on the screen relative to the distance and speed with which you move the mouse. Increasing the pointer speed makes the mouse move further in relation to how far you actually move the mouse.

131

pointer trails If you have trouble following the mouse pointer on your screen, you can turn on pointer trails to make it more visible. As you drag the mouse, multiple copies of the pointer trail behind the actual pointer to emphasize the mouse movement.

> You can adjust the mouse pointer speed and turn pointer trails on and off under Windows 95 and 98. Choose Start | Settings | Control Panel. Double-click the mouse icon, then click the Motion tab to display its options (Figure P.4). Make your choices and click OK to apply them.

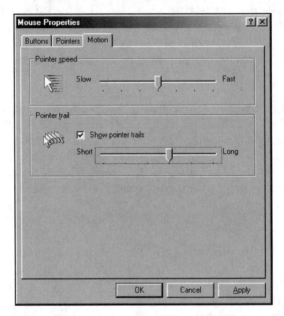

Figure P.4 You can adjust the mouse pointer speed and trails on this dialog box tab.

pointing device Any device you can connect to the computer and use to move the mouse pointer on the screen, including a mouse, trackball, touchpad, joystick, or pen.

POP POP stands for Post Office Protocol and identifies a particular type of server on the Internet that manages your incoming e-mail messages. Your e-mail program connects to the ISP's POP (or POP3) server to retrieve your e-mail messages. (See also *server*.)

port Devices plug into a receptacle, or port, on your computer. Most ports are part of an adapter card within the computer. (See also *parallel port, serial port,* and *USB*.)

132

Computer & Internet Dictionary

portrait orientation A tall page format that turns the page so the longer side runs along the side edge. Portrait orientation fits less information on each line or row of the document, but fits more lines of information per page. (See also *landscape orientation*.)

POST Your computer executes the POST (Power-On Self Test) each time it boots. It includes a number of tests for the CPU, the RAM, the hard disks, and other devices connected to the system. If any circuit fails its POST test, the system displays an error message.

post The term post applies in two cases when online. When you copy a new Web page or Web site to a Web server computer so that other users can view the Web page or site, you are posting the site. When you add a new message to a newsgroup for other users to read, you are posting the message.

PostScript The PostScript page description language enables printers and other high-quality reproduction devices (like a Linotronic typesetting device) to print high-quality text and graphics. Only PostScript-capable printers and devices can print PostScript information. However, any PostScript-capable device can print an Encapsulated PostScript (.EPS) file, no matter what application was used to create the file.

power down When you turn a device's power off, it powers down.

> If you power down a device to turn it off and then restart it, listen for the device to power down all the way before powering it back up. This ensures that any moving parts within the device have stopped before you reapply power.

power up When you turn a device's power on, it powers up.

power supply The computer's power supply device covers AC power from the wall socket to DC power for the computer's use.

power surge A power surge occurs when the power voltage increases substantially on the power lines coming into your home or within your home. This sudden power increase, or spike, can zap parts within your computer and cause damage. (See also *surge protector*.)

PowerPoint Microsoft sells the PowerPoint presentation graphics program both as an individual program and as part of the Microsoft Office suite. PowerPoint can import information from Word and Excel and offers a number of features for creating multimedia presentations.

133

ppm This acronym for pages per minute helps you compare the relative speeds of different kinds of printers. For a faster printer, look for one that prints a higher number of pages per minute.

PPP PPP stands for Point-to-Point Protocol, a protocol your system uses (along with TCP/IP) to connect to the Internet via a phone line. Most ISPs use PPP servers (often based on the Windows NT Server network operating system). (See also *Dial-Up Networking, ISP,* and *SLIP*.)

precedence When a spreadsheet program calculates a formula, it uses precedence (also called the order of precedence) to determine the order in which the formula should be calculated. Most spreadsheets first perform exponentiation (^), then multiplication (*) and division (/), then addition (+) and subtraction (-). When operators have the same precedence, the spreadsheet program calculates the formula from left to right. (See also *operators*.)

presentation graphics program A presentation graphics program creates pages similar to slides in a slide show. Each page, or slide, in the presentation has a title and either a bulleted list, chart, or graphic. Current presentation graphics programs can display the presentation information as an on-screen show. Also, you can print the presentation information in a variety of formats: page by page, as speaker note pages, or as handouts showing multiple slides. Finally, most presentation graphics programs make it possible to send a presentation to a company that will output the presentation information as 35mm slides.

print To send a file's information to the printer, which then creates some type of hard copy output. In most applications, you choose the File|Print command to print.

print buffer A temporary storage area that holds the print queue (information being sent to the printer) until the printer is ready to accept it. Most printers have built-in memory, but a printer may not have enough memory to hold multiple print jobs or to print very large files.

print job When you choose File|Print, set printing options, and then click OK to send a file to the printer, you create a print job for the printer to handle. A single print job may print one or many copies of a file.

> In Windows 95 and 98, a printer icon appears in the system tray area at the right end of the taskbar when you send one or more print jobs to the printer. Double-click that icon to open a window where you can pause and cancel print jobs.

Print Screen key When you press the Print Screen key in Windows 95 and 98, a graphical copy of the information shown on your screen is to sent the Clipboard. You can paste the image from the Clipboard into a graphics program to save it as a file.

print preview Many applications offer a print preview feature (Figure P.5) so that you can see how a file will appear when you print it. Print preview helps you ensure that pages break correctly. Also check margin size and overall positioning of text and graphics. You can choose the File|Print Preview command in most applications to display the print preview.

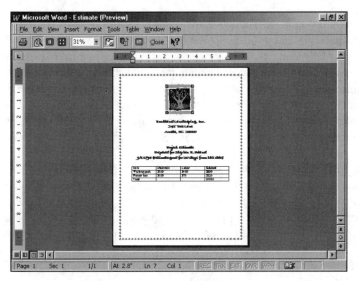

Figure P.5 The print preview feature in an application shows you how your file printout will look.

printer A printer connected to your computer makes a hard copy of any file that you specify. The type of printer you connect and install for your system controls your printing options. For example, the type of printer determines the paper size you can use to print. (See also *dot-matrix printer*, *inkjet printer*, and *laser printer*.)

printer driver You install printer driver software for your printer to enable Windows to control the printer and its features. Windows comes with drivers for a number of printers, but new printers also include a floppy disk or CD-ROM from which you can install the printer drivers.

135

printer font A printer font is installed in a special module in the printer to help the printer to print that font more effectively. If your system doesn't have a matching screen font installed, you won't be able to see what the printer font looks like until printing the document. Most systems and printers today avoid this complication by using TrueType fonts. (See also *font, screen font,* and *TrueType font.*)

printer port A port through which you connect a printer to your PC. Most printers connect to a PC via a parallel port, but some can connect via a serial port. (See also *parallel port* and *serial port.*)

program A program, also called software or an application, is a fixed collection of instructions that your computer can understand and execute. Each program falls into a particular category and performs a particular function. Some programs serve a very specific purpose, such as a utility program that compresses and extracts files. Other programs offer features that handle a broad variety of tasks. For example, a word processor enables you to enter, format, save, and print documents. You must install a program on your computer for the computer to use it. (See also *freeware* and *shareware.*)

programming language A set of vocabulary, grammar, syntax (command structure rules), organization, style rules, and tools a programmer uses to create programs. Low-level languages can directly control the CPU, but are harder to learn and use. High-level languages use more English-like keywords and also don't require the programmer to control areas directly in the CPU. Fortran, C++, Visual Basic, Visual C++, and Visual J++ are all high-level programming languages.

Project The Microsoft Project project management software allows a user to plan the schedule for a project and monitor project progress. In Project, you break a project up into tasks, assign each task to a resource (person, equipment, or outside contractor), set a start and finish date for each task, allocate an amount of work (actual completion time) for each task, and apply a budget amount for each task. As time passes, you enter actual work, budget, and deadline information to compare progress to the original plan.

promote To shift a selection to a higher outline (heading) level using a program's outlining feature.

prompt A prompt indicates that a program is waiting for you to perform an action or provide further information. The DOS prompt is a string of characters that typically looks like this: C:\>. You type a DOS command at a DOS prompt and press [Enter] to proceed. Windows programs often display a message box to prompt you. For example, a message box might ask if you want to continue an operation; click Yes to do so.

properties In Windows, you set properties to specify the performance of a particular feature. For example, the Display Properties dialog box will display wallpaper or a pattern on the desktop or control how many colors Windows displays. To access the properties for something in Windows, right-click it and then click the Properties choice.

protection Add protection to a file to prevent someone from making unauthorized changes to it. For example, many software programs enable you to password-protect a file; you can add a password to a file to prevent anyone else from opening it or editing it. You also can mark a file as read only in Windows to prevent inadvertent changes to it. Finally, if your system is connected to a network, you can control whether other users can merely open a file or also make changes to it, and assign passwords as needed. (See also *read only*.)

> To set protection options for a shared disk or folder, right-click the disk or folder icon in the My Computer or Windows Explorer window, then click Sharing. Make your changes on the Sharing tab, and click OK.

protocol The rules and standards two devices must follow to communicate via modem, LAN connection, or Internet connection. For example, the underlying protocol used on the Internet is TCP/IP. (See also *TCP/IP*.)

public domain Information in the public domain is not protected by copyright, so you can download and use it freely. To use information protected by copyright, in contrast, you need to obtain permission from its author and pay any needed fees. For example, freeware software is in the public domain, so you can download it for free. Shareware programs, on the other hand, are not public domain. When you download text, graphics, sounds, or other items from the Internet, make sure it's in the public domain before you use it. (See also *freeware* and *shareware*.)

publish To transform information from a basic file into a final, formatted document including graphics and page layout features like headers and footers. When you publish a Web page or a Web site, you copy it to a Web server computer in your company or from an ISP. After you publish your page or site, other users can display it using Web browser software.

137

Publisher This inexpensive, entry-level page layout (desktop publishing) program from Microsoft allows you to create a variety of documents such as post cards (Figure P.6), newsletters, and flyers. Publisher offers a number of wizards to lead beginners through the process of selecting and applying a document design.

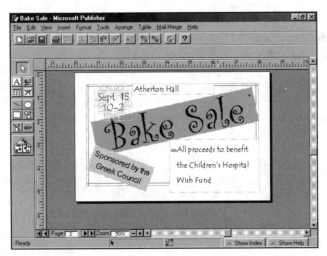

Figure P.6 Create attractive brochures and newsletters with Publisher.

pull-down menu This is another name for menus in Windows programs. Commands appear on a menu below the menu bar, as if you had pulled down the menu to open it.

push content Web sites offering push content work in conjunction with channels in Internet Explorer 4.0 and the Netcaster feature in Netscape Communicator. After choosing the channels or sites from which you want to receive information, the Web sites automatically deliver, or push, that information to your system. You can read the stored information at your convenience.

Q

QuarkXPress (pronounced quark express) This professional page layout (desktop publishing) program competes with Adobe PageMaker. Quark has long excelled in preparing documents for four-color printing, such as magazine layouts and ads. PageMaker is more suited for long documents, but Quark has substantially improved its long document features. (See also *PageMaker*.)

query You perform a query in a database program to find and retrieve matching entries in the database. You enter criteria, and the database displays all the records that match. For example, if you have a long customer list database, you can create a query listing only customers living in a particular ZIP code. You also can enter query instructions when you perform a mail merge. Some spreadsheet programs enable you to perform a query to hide non-matching items listed in the spreadsheet. Finally, if you use a Web page to search for information, the page performs a query in a database on the Web server to match the information that you requested.

queue (pronounced q) A queue holds instructions or files waiting to be executed or printed.

Quick Launch toolbar This new toolbar (Figure Q.1) appears by default on the Windows 98 taskbar or on machines with IE4, near the Start button. From left to right, it offers buttons for starting Internet Explorer, starting Outlook Express, minimizing open windows, and viewing available Web channels.

Figure Q.1 You may want to start certain programs using the Quick Launch toolbar.

Quicken Quicken (Figure Q.2) is the leading personal accounting software on the market. With Quicken, you can enter and print checks, categorize how you spend and make money, display helpful reports, or even pay your bills and retrieve bank account transaction information over the Internet. (See also *accounting software*.)

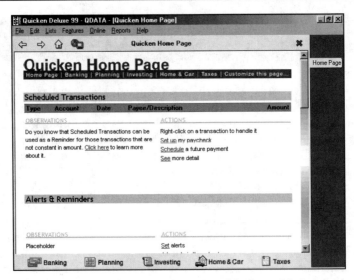

Figure Q.2 Manage your checkbook and budget with Quicken.

QuickTime QuickTime software enables your system to play movies stored in the QuickTime file format.

quit To exit a program. In most programs, you choose the File|Exit commnad to exit the program, but other programs may use a File|Quit command or display a Quit button that you can click to exit the program.

R

ragged right When aligning paragraphs of text in a word processor flush left, the right sides of the lines do not line up because the lines tend to be unequal in length. This yields a ragged appearance along the right side of each paragraph. (See also *flush left, flush right*.)

RAM (see memory)

range In a spreadsheet program, a range is a contiguous block of cells. For example, the block of cells that spans from cell C5 in the upper-left corner to cell G10 in the lower-right corner forms the range C5:G10. A range also may refer to a contiguous set of items in other applications, such as a range of pages to print from a word processing document or a range of records from a database.

read When a computer reads information, it retrieves the information from a disk into the system's RAM.

read-only When you mark a file as read-only, you are able to open the file but not change it.

To mark a file as read-only, right-click the file icon in the My Computer or Windows Explorer window, then click Properties. Click the Read-only check box on the General tab, and click OK.

read/write head A device within a disk drive that floats just above the disk surface and reads and writes information on the disk surface. To write information, the read/write head changes magnetic information on the disk.

Read Me file A program or software component typically comes with a Read Me file that contains necessary information from the software publisher. The Read Me file may be named *Readme.wri*, *Readme.txt*, or simply *Read.me*.

You should always read the Read Me file for a new program, preferably before you install the program.

reboot To restart the computer, especially after you experience a problem with it or install a new piece of hardware or software. (See also *cold boot, restart,* and *warm boot*.)

141

recalculation In a spreadsheet program, recalculation updates formula results after you change entries in related cells. Most spreadsheet programs recalculate automatically. In Excel, you can manually recalculate the spreadsheet by pressing [F9].

record (pronounced reck-ord) In a database program, a record represents one full entry. For example, if you create a database to list all your audio CDs, the full entry for each CD (including the *Title, Artist, Release Date,* and *Price* fields) forms a record. (See also *database* and *field*.)

record (pronounced ree-cord) Using sound or video software to capture digital sound or video. For example, you can use Windows Sound Recorder to record your voice from a microphone.

To start Sound Recorder, choose Start | Programs | Accessories | Multimedia | Sound Recorder (Windows 95) or Start | Programs | Accessories | Entertainment | Sound Recorder (Windows 98).

Recycle Bin The Recycle Bin in Windows (Figure R.1) holds files that you've deleted from the hard disk. The files remain in the Recycle Bin in case you need to restore them. You can permanently delete the files from the Recycle Bin by right-clicking the Recycle Bin icon on the desktop and then clicking Empty Recycle Bin.

The Recycle Bin icon looks like an empty waste can when there are no files in the Recycle Bin folder. The icon changes to a waste can holding crumpled paper when it is holding some files.

Figure R.1 The Recycle Bin stores deleted files until you choose to delete them permanently.

142

Redo Recent versions of many Microsoft Office programs offer a Redo command so that you can reinstate a change you previously reversed using the Undo command. (See also *undo*.)

refresh Most Web browsers offer a Refresh button. Click the Refresh button to reload a Web page that didn't display completely or correctly on your system. You also can press [F5] to refresh any open My Computer or Windows Explorer window in Windows 95 or 98 if it doesn't automatically display recent changes.

refresh rate Every monitor redraws the screen information at a regular interval called the refresh rate. The faster the refresh rate, the smoother and more flicker-free the display appears.

Registry The Windows Registry (in 95, 98, and NT) stores account information, communication protocol information, Windows settings, software settings, and other preference information. The Registry actually consists of two files, *SYSTEM.DAT* and *USER.DAT*.

> You can manually edit the Registry using the Windows Registry Editor, but you should only do so if you're working with a tech support person or have specific instructions on what to do. If the Registry becomes damaged, your system may not boot properly.

relative reference In a spreadsheet program, the relative reference in a formula changes if you copy the formula to another location. The relative cell address in the formula refers to a cell in a position relative to the formula, not the specific cell. For example, if you enter the formula =SUM(F4:F9) into cell F10, the formula references the six cells directly above the cell holding it. If you then copy the formula from cell F10 to cell G10, the formula changes to =SUM(G4:G9). The copied formula references the six cells directly above the cell holding it. (See also *absolute reference* and *address*.)

REM You enter the *REM* (short for "remark") command at the beginning of a line in a DOS batch file (like *AUTOEXEC.BAT* or *CONFIG.SYS*) to tell DOS not to execute the instructions in the line. If you later want to reinstate the line, delete the REM. To enter a remark in a Windows .INI file, enter an asterisk at the beginning of the line. To enter a remark in a programming environment, use another symbol or character, such as the apostrophe.

> To edit *AUTOEXEC.BAT* and *CONFIG.SYS*, use the System Configuration Editor. Choose Start | Run. Type **sysedit** in the Open text box, then click OK. Make your changes to each file, save the file, then close the System Configuration Editor.

143

removable disk Also called removable storage, a removable disk drive reads and writes information to a removable cartridge or disk holding a large quantity of information (about 100M to 2G). You can move removable disks in and out of the drive, much as you would a floppy disk.

replace When you use the wrong term or value in a file, you can replace every instance of the term or value with another term or value that you specify. For example, you can replace all references to *Mike* with *Michael*. You accomplish this with a search and replace operation. (See also *search and replace*.)

reply When you receive an e-mail message, you can click the Reply button in your e-mail program to write a message in response to the received message. The reply message often includes the text of the received message so that your recipient will know to what you're replying. You can also post replies to messages posted on a newsgroup.

> Many e-mail programs include a Reply to All command or button. Clicking it automatically addresses your response message to the person who originally e-mailed you and to any other recipients copied on that earlier message.

report In a database program, you create a report to view or print the data in a nicely-designed page format rather than in a plain table. In many database programs, you can add special report fields that calculate information, as well.

reset If you need to restart your system because Windows has stopped working or has displayed an error message, you can press the Reset button. The Reset button performs a warm boot. You can use the Reset button if you can't use a command or keyboard combination to restart the system. (See also *warm boot*.)

resolution The resolution for an image or computer screen indicates how large or detailed the image is or how detailed the on-screen display is. Resolution is expressed in pixels. When you set your monitor to display at 800x600, the screen displays 800 pixels across and 600 vertically. A higher resolution display uses more, smaller pixels, yielding a crisper picture. Likewise, a higher resolution image has more pixels, so you can display the image at a larger size. In contrast, if you increase the size of an image with lower resolution, it can become distorted. (See also *dots per inch* and *pixel*.)

restart Windows 95 and 98 offer a command to restart the system. Choose Start|Shut Down. Click Restart the computer? and then Yes (Windows 95) or Restart and then OK (Windows 98) in the Shut Down Windows dialog box. (See also *warm boot*.)

restore To reduce the size of a file or application window so that it doesn't fill the desktop or the working area within the application window. When you restore a window, you can resize the window or drag its title bar to move it.

Restore button One of three buttons at the right end of the title bar for a file window or application window. The Restore button has two small overlapping windows on it. You can click the Restore button to return the window to its previous size before it was maximized to full screen size. When the window is restored, the Restore button changes to the Maximize button. (See also *Maximize button*.)

revision marks Revision marking in a word processing document (and now in some spreadsheet and presentation graphics programs) shows the changes made to a file using markings like those in Figure R.2. The revision marking, or change tracking, feature uses a different color or style to identify changes made by each different colleague or editor with whom you share the file. You can then review each change and decide whether to accept or reject it.

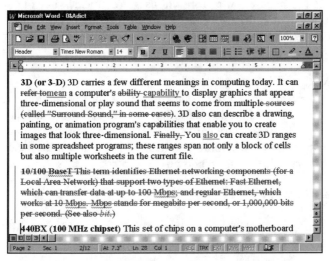

Figure R.2 Turn on revision marking so a document's author can view your changes.

RGB Your computer monitor displays in RGB color. That is, it displays beams of red, green, and blue light with varying intensity to yield other colors in the spectrum. In professional graphics, converting images from the RGB spectrum used in computing to the four colors used for color printing (called process colors) can sometimes alter an image's overall tone and appearance.

Rich Text Format Files that contain not only the basic data but also basic formatting such as fonts and font sizes. Most word processors and some other types of programs can open .RTF files, allowing you to share information between programs more easily .

right align Aligning information against the right margin, the right side of the cell, or the right side of an object. Right alignment yields an uneven appearance at the left side of a block of text, called ragged left. (See also *alignment* and *flush left, flush right*.)

right-click To move the mouse pointer over an on-screen item and press and release the right mouse button once.

You generally click using the left mouse button unless a program instruction tells you to do otherwise or you want to display a shortcut menu.

RISC (pronounced risk) RISC stands for Reduced Instruction Set Computer, a type of microprocessor. Because these processors have been optimized to handle fewer instructions more quickly, they operate much more quickly than the CISC (Complex Instruction Set Computer) chips powering Windows-based PCs. You may find RISC chips running some computers and other hardware.

RJ-11 Short for Registered Jack-11, this is more commonly called a phone jack. Internal modems also have an RJ-11 port, which accommodates the small four- or six-wire cords (cables) used to connect phone components in the U.S. Some LANs use RJ-11 connections and cabling, but many Ethernet LANs use eight-wire RJ-45 connectors.

ROM (see memory)

root The first or top-level folder holding all other folders on a disk. The root for disk C: is C:\. The root for disk A: is A:\.

ROTFL This acronym stands for "Rolling On The Floor Laughing." Use it in an e-mail message or newsgroup posting to express your appreciation for someone else's humor.

router Special hardware or software that connects two networks, usually LANs using the same protocols.

row A row in a table or spreadsheet consists of all the cells on one horizontal line across the table or spreadsheet.

 To select an entire row in a spreadsheet program, you generally can click the row number at the left side. Drag across multiple row numbers to select multiple rows.

RS-232 This standard applies to serial ports and governs how they transmit data. You can connect an external modem to an RS-232-compatible serial port. (See also *serial port*.)

run To start or load a program, or to execute a macro in a program.

sans serif A font lacking serifs (decorative cross strokes) on the letters, like **Arial, Gill Sans, Impact**, or **Helvetica**. (See also *serif*.)

save To name and store a file in a folder on a disk. After making any changes in a file, you should save it again to include those changes in the stored version on file. In most applications, the File|Save command or a Save button on a toolbar will save the current file.

ScanDisk Windows 95 and 98 include a utility program called ScanDisk (Figure S.1) that can correct some disk errors, such as when you try to copy a file from a floppy disk and see an error message that Windows can't read from the disk. To start ScanDisk, choose Start|Programs|Accessories|System Tools|ScanDisk.

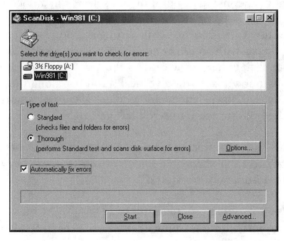

Figure S.1 The Windows ScanDisk utility can repair common disk problems.

scanner A device that uses light to read an image from a hard copy, such as a photo, in order to convert it to a digital format that you can save on disk, edit, and print.

Most scanner models today connect via the parallel port. However, if you have Windows 98 and a system with a USB port, you may want consider a newer scanner model that connects via the USB port.

149

screen area (see resolution)

screen font A screen font represents a printer font on the screen, so the document display will more closely match the printed result. (See also *font, printer font,* and *TrueType font.*)

screen saver A screen saver displays an on-screen moving image after your computer has been idle for a specified period of time. Monitors originally needed screen savers to prevent images from "burning in" to the display material and leaving permanent ghost images. With improved monitors, screen savers are more of a way to personalize PCs. Windows comes with some screen savers; you also can download or purchase other screen savers.

scroll When you scroll a file, you change the portion of the file that's visible on the screen. For example, if you scroll down in a spreadsheet, you display the group of cells below the previously displayed cells. You also can scroll a list in a dialog box to display other options in the list. Note that scrolling does not move the insertion point or cell selector in a document.

scroll bar You use a scroll bar to scroll through a file. Each scroll bar appears as a long gray bar with an arrow at either end and a scroll box within the bar. You can click either arrow or drag the scroll box to scroll. An application window may offer a vertical scroll bar along the right side; use it to scroll up and down. The window might also offer a horizontal scroll bar along the bottom; use it to scroll left and right.

scroll box This dark gray box appears on a scroll bar. Click on either side of the scroll box to scroll through a screen of information. Drag the scroll box to scroll the document more quickly.

Scroll Lock key In some programs, pressing [Scroll Lock] will let you use the arrow keys to scroll through a document rather than to move the insertion point or cell selector.

SCSI (pronounced scuzzy) SCSI stands for Small Computer System Interface, and connects devices like hard disks, removable disk drives, CD-ROM drives, and scanners to a PC. If you install a SCSI adapter card into your system, you can "daisy chain" a number of SCSI devices, making it much easier to add devices to your system. That is, you plug the first device into the port on the adapter, plug the next device into the first one, and so on. Following are some SCSI variations that you might encounter:

- SCSI-2. Handles 8 bits of data at a 4MBps transfer rate, and uses a 50-pin connector.
- Wide SCSI. Uses a 68-pin cable, handling 16 bits of data.

Computer & Internet Dictionary

- Fast SCSI. Transfers at up to 10 MBps (8-bit).
- Fast Wide SCSI. Transfers data at rates up to 20 MBps (16-bit).
- Ultra Wide SCSI. Transfers data a rates up to 40 MBps (16-bit).
- Wide Ultra2 SCSI. Transfers data at rates up to 80 MBps.

SDRAM SDRAM stands for Synchronous DRAM, RAM that operates three times faster than conventional types of RAM and nearly twice as fast as EDO RAM. It synchronizes its operations with the CPU's operations, thus working more efficiently. Because SDRAM can work at up to 100 MHz, it can also accommodate the speed of the 440BX (100 MHz) chipset and system bus used in today's fastest systems.

search When you want to look for a particular word, phrase, or value in a word processor, spreadsheet, database, or presentation graphics program, you can perform a search, or a find, to identify matching instances of the word or value. When you're working on the Web, you can perform a search to find Web pages that mention the topic you specify. A Web search engine site will perform a Web search. (See also *find* and *search engine*.)

search and replace To find a match for a term that you specify and replace the match with other specified information. This feature, called search and replace, or find and replace (Figure S.2), helps save time when correcting a repeated mistake in a document. You can replace only selected matching instances of a term, or all instances. To start a search and replace operation, choose the Edit|Replace command.
(See also *find*, *replace*, and *search*.)

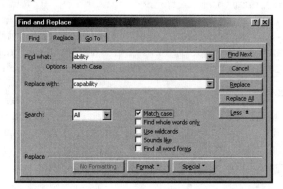

Figure S.2 Use the search and replace feature to replace information throughout a file.

search engine A Web site that performs a search of Web pages (and in some cases, newsgroups), to find pages with information concerning a specific topic. The search engine displays a listing of links to the pages covering the topic. Click a link to go to one of the listed pages. Each search engine keeps an index of pages registered by Web site operators and uses a slightly different method of matching terms. (See also *search string*.)

> Most Web browsers now offer a Search button. Click it to see a listing of popular search engines, such as excite (*http://www.excite.com*), Yahoo! (*http://www.yahoo.com*), and Lycos (*http://www.lycos.com*).

search string A term or phrase you want the application or search engine to find. Depending on the type of operation, application, or search engine you're using, you may need to follow particular rules (syntax) when you enter the search string. For example, if your search string includes multiple words, they may need to be enclosed in quotation marks.

sector Computer disks hold concentric tracks of information; a sector is a small segment of a track. One or more sectors form a cluster on the disk. (See also *cluster*.)

security When you connect to the Web, online service, or a LAN, information downloads to your system. Any incoming information could carry a virus that would infect your computer, and many connections provide hackers with the opportunity to access your system information or intercept transmissions. Security measures can help prevent damage to your system information or disclosure of confidential information. You can use security features in applications to protect files, check for viruses, use digital (security) certificates, and use other techniques to ensure your system's security. (See also *antivirus, digital certificate, password,* and *virus*.)

seek time The seek time indicates the average amount of time it takes for the read/write head of a disk drive to move over the requested sector on the disk. Seek time is measured in microseconds (ms), with smaller measurements indicating faster drives. Current disk drives have a seek time of as little as 7.5ms. (See also *read/write head* and *sector*.)

select To highlight text or cells in a file by dragging the insertion point over them, or to click on an object or window. Selection handles appear around a selected object. Any command or action that you perform applies to the current selection.

self-extracting Normally, you need the right compression utility to extract the files within a compressed file or archive. However, if you are sending an archive to someone without the necessary utility program, you can create a self-extracting archive using the compression utility. A self-extracting archive is an executable (*.EXE*) file. The user can double-click the .EXE file in a My Computer or Windows Explorer window to run the file and extract the files it holds. (See also *compressed file, extract,* and *WinZip.*)

semiconductor Integrated circuits and other computer components use semiconductor material (typically silicon or germanium). The semiconductor usually serves to separate the electrical conductors in the circuit.

serial port A serial port transmits asynchronous data in serial fashion (one bit after another), unlike a parallel port, which can transmit data in multiple parallel streams. An external modem or a mouse might be plugged into a serial port. (See also *asynchronous, parallel port, RS-232,* and *UART.*)

serial cable A serial cable connects a device to the system's serial port. A serial cable usually has smaller connectors (9-pin) than a parallel cable (25-pin). You should make sure you buy a serial cable that matches the connectors for the device you're connecting.

serif A decorative cross stroke that finishes off the ends of certain letters, such as the bottom of a lowercase "l" or "f." Serif fonts like **Bookman Old Style**, **Palatino**, and **Times New Roman** work well as body fonts. (See also *sans serif.*)

server A server computer is the central control point on a LAN (local area network), and stores the networking software and central resources shared by other computers connected to the network. On the Internet, a server computer stores and manages a particular type of information. For example, a Web server stores and transmits Web pages. (See also *dedicated file server, mail server,* and *newsgroup server.*)

setting A choice that you make to control how a program operates or how a command executes. For example, dialog boxes offer settings in programs.

setup Most applications come with a setup program (usually named *SETUP.EXE* or *INSTALL.EXE*) to install the application on your computer.

> When you insert the CD-ROM for a new application, your system usually finds and runs the setup program automatically. If not, open My Computer, double-click the icon for the CD-ROM drive, then double-click the *SETUP.EXE* or *INSTALL.EXE* file icon.

153

shareware You can download shareware programs from the Internet and other online resources, or find them on sampler CD-ROMs that come with magazines and books. Shareware software operates on the honor system. If you decide you like the shareware and want to continue using it, you need to register it and pay a small fee to the shareware author. (See also *freeware*.)

Shift key Pressing [Shift] on the keyboard in conjunction with another key types a capital letter or a shifted character like @ or *. [Shift] may also be part of a shortcut key combination that performs a command or action. (See *Shift+arrow*.)

Shift+arrow To select information in a word processor or other application, press and hold [Shift] while repeatedly pressing an arrow key [←] [→] [↑] [↓].

Shift-click Press and hold [Shift] while clicking something on the screen. In a word processor, you can click at the beginning of a block of text to select, then Shift-click at the end of the block to finish the selection.

shortcut menu A shortcut menu, also called a context menu, offers commands that apply to the operation at hand. To display a shortcut menu (Figure S.3), right-click selected text or a selected object. (See also *submenu*.)

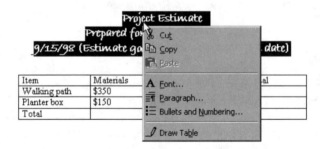

Figure S.3 Right-click a selection to see a shortcut menu of commands.

shut down Before you turn off your PC, you should shut down Windows 95 or 98. Choose Start|Shut Down. In Windows 95, choose Shut Down the Computer?, then click Yes. In Windows 98, choose Shut Down, then click OK. When the screen displays the message It's Now Safe To Turn Off Your Computer, you can turn off the computer's power.

Computer & Internet Dictionary

signature Your e-mail program or newsreader software can insert signature lines at the end of every message you send or post to save you the trouble of typing your contact information at the end of every message. Your digital signature also may include ASCII art. (See also *ASCII art*.)

SIMM SIMM (Single Inline Memory Module) holds RAM. SIMMs plug into sockets on the motherboard or another card and come in two formats: 30-pin and 72-pin. If you're adding memory to an older system, you must buy the right kind of SIMM. (See also *DIMM*.)

site license A software purchase agreement that enables the purchaser to install the software on a limited number of PCs. The purchaser receives a discounted price for each "copy" of the software used, so purchasing a site license results in significant savings over purchasing multiple individual copies of the software. Software publishers offer site licenses to discourage software piracy, such as illegally installing a program on numerous PCs.

SLIP SLIP stands for Serial Line Internet Protocol, a protocol your system can use (along with TCP/IP) to connect to the Internet via a phone line. Some older UNIX servers on the Internet enable users to connect only via a SLIP connection. (See also *Dial-Up Networking* and *PPP*.)

slot Also called an expansion slot, this is a type of long socket on a motherboard (or other system board) into which you plug an adapter card to add a new device to the system. The number and type of available slots on a system determines how many devices you can add (unless you're adding USB or FireWire devices). Most newer systems come with five or six open slots: two to three ISA slots and three PCI slots. (See also *adapter*.)

small caps Words displayed in all capital letters using special smaller-sized capital letters, LIKE THIS. You apply small caps via a formatting selection within an application. Word processors and presentation graphics programs may offer small caps formatting, but some types of applications do not. To apply small caps in Word, for example, choose Format|Font, click to check the Small Caps check box on the Font tab, then click OK. (See also *all caps*.)

SmartSuite This group of complementary programs from Lotus Development Corp. competes with the Microsoft Office Suite. The current SmartSuite package, called the Millennium Edition, includes Lotus 1-2-3 (spreadsheet), Word Pro (word processor), Freelance Graphics (presentation graphics), Approach (database), Organizer (PIM), ScreenCam (captures voice and on-screen actions), and FastSite (a new Web-site development tool).

smiley (see emoticon)

SMTP SMTP stands for Simple Mail Transfer Protocol and identifies the server at your ISP that manages your outgoing e-mail messages. Your e-mail program connects to the ISP's SMTP server to send your e-mail messages to recipients. (See also *ISP* and *POP*.)

snail mail Regular paper mail, which travels at a snail's pace when compared with e-mail.

soft hyphen Also called an optional hyphen. You insert a soft hyphen into a word that appears near the end of the line. (In Word, press [Ctrl]+[-] to insert a soft hyphen.) If you make a change prior to the word with the soft hyphen that will cause it to wrap to the next line, the application will hyphenate the word at the soft hyphen location and only wrap part of it to the next line. Use soft hyphens to avoid short lines of text in a document.

> In the current version of Word, you can use the Tools | Language | Hyphenation command to have Word hyphenate a document automatically.

soft page break An application inserts a soft, or automatic, page break whenever you enter enough information to fill the current page. (See also *hard page break*.)

software (see program)

SOHO SOHO stands for Small Office Home Office. It refers to products, such as combination printer/scanner/fax devices, designed specifically for small businesses or businesses run from the home. Products for the SOHO market typically save on both space and money.

sort When you sort information, you place it in a new order. You can sort tables and lists in a word processor document, lists of entries in a spreadsheet, or records in a database. Choose a column or field of information by which to sort, as well as a particular sort order. For example, you could sort a list of names and address as in A–Z order by last name. (See also *ascending order* and *descending order*.)

Sound Recorder You can use this Windows applet to record and save sounds if your PC has a sound card and microphone. Sound Recorder saves files as .WAV sound files. To start Sound Recorder, choose Start | Programs | Accessories | Multimedia | Sound Recorder (Windows 95) or Start | Programs | Accessories | Entertainment | Sound Recorder (Windows 98). (See also *.WAV*.)

Computer & Internet Dictionary

Sound recorder can record sounds using Telephone quality (11KHz, 8-bit, mono), Radio quality (22KHz, 8-bit, mono), or CD quality (44KHz, 16-bit, stereo). You can choose the sound quality by choosing Edit | Audio Properties. Make your choice from the Preferred Quality choice in the Recording area, and click OK. The higher the quality, the larger the file. If you plan to include your file on a Web site, choose a lower quality.

source An original file or selection that you're copying, or the location from which you copy or move a file or selection. (See also *destination*.)

source code High-level programming languages usually use a two-step process. First, the programmer writes code (programming instructions) using the programming language. These original instructions are called the source code. Then, the programmer runs a compiler program to translate the source code into machine instructions that the computer understands; the compiler also packs the compiled instructions into an .EXE (executable) file. (See also *programming language*.)

space character Enter a space character to separate words and sentences.

You may have learned in typing class to enter two space characters after each sentence. That is no longer necessary because the font designs compress the space between letters within words, which makes a single space after a sentence a large enough break.

Spacebar Pressing the Spacebar key, the long key at the bottom of the keyboard, inserts a space character. Note that some keyboards have a divided Spacebar button, with the right half working like the traditional Spacebar key and the left half working like the backspace key. (See also *Backspace key*.)

spam Spam, the electronic equivalent of junk mail, is any unsolicited advertisement sent via e-mail or posted on a newsgroup. Savvy Net citizens frown on junk mail, because it annoys recipients and clogs up Internet traffic. A spammer might send thousands of messages at a time, leading the spammer to lose his or her ISP account.

spelling checker A tool that can check the spelling of every word or entry in a file. The spelling checker compares each word to a dictionary and highlights any word that doesn't match an existing dictionary entry (Figure S.4). You can then decide whether or not the word needs correcting. (See also *grammar checker*.)

157

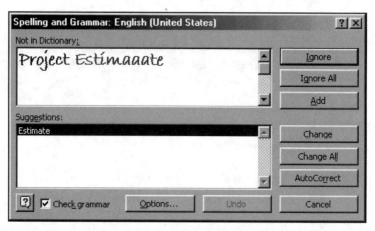

Figure S.4 A spelling checker highlights your spelling errors and suggests a replacement.

spinner buttons Spinner buttons, also called increment buttons, appear in a dialog box next to a text box holding a value. Clicking the up spinner button (it has an upward-pointing triangle) will increase the value in the text box. Clicking the down spinner button (it has a downward-pointing triangle) will decrease the value in the text box. (See also *dialog box*.)

spooler A spooler feature works in conjunction with an application to transfer information from a program to RAM or to a temporary file on disk, from which it can be printed or processed. For example, the Background Printing feature in Word is a spooler that moves file information from one area of RAM to another before sending it to the printer. This frees up the RAM that Word uses for its regular work so that you can use Word while a document prints, something you couldn't do in earlier versions of Word.

spreadsheet A spreadsheet program presents a grid of columns and rows that intersect to form cells. You can enter text (labels), a date, a value, or a formula in each cell. A spreadsheet formula includes mathematical operators to perform a calculation. (See also *cell*, *Excel*, *formula*, *function*, *Lotus 1-2-3*, and *operator*.)

SQL SQL stands for Structured Query Language. You can use SQL commands to query nearly any type of relational database, especially those stored on large mainframe computers. SQL queries use some natural language commands like SELECT and DELETE. Query results usually appear in a table format; the information can be copied and pasted into a word processor or spreadsheet. (See also *database*.)

Start menu In Windows 95 and Windows 98, the Start menu serves as the main avenue for starting programs and accessing Windows features. To open the Start menu, click the Start button at the far left end of the taskbar.

Computer & Internet Dictionary

start page The first page your Web browser loads when it connects to the World Wide Web. (See also *browser software* and *home page*.)

> To select a new start page in Internet Explorer 4.0, display the page that you want to use as the start page. Choose View | Internet Options. Click the Use Current button in the Home Page area of the General tab, then click OK.
>
> To start a new start page in Netscape Communicator, choose Edit | Preferences. Enter the Web address in the location area, then click OK.

start up To boot up your computer. When you start the computer, it performs a number of steps, such as loading Windows, and displaying the desktop. (See also *boot* and *POST*.)

startup disk With Windows 95 and 98, you can create a startup disk by loading a floppy disk with the key system files. You can use it to start your system if it won't boot from the hard disk. Insert the startup disk in the floppy disk drive, then power up the computer. The system reads the system files on the startup disk and boots to the DOS prompt. (See also *prompt*.)

> To create a startup disk, choose Start | Settings | Control Panel. Double-click the Add/Remove Programs icon, then click the Startup Disk tab. Insert a floppy disk into the disk drive, and click Create Disk.

status bar The bottom of the application window in many programs has a status bar. The status bar often displays information about the open file, such as how many pages it has and the current page number. In some cases, the status bar includes tools you can use to work on the file. For example, the Word Pro status bar offers buttons for formatting text.

storage Storage is another name for disk space, the area where you store files created in applications. You may see a disk drive called a storage device. (See also *memory*.)

style A style includes a number of formatting settings, such as the font, font size, and alignment. Instead of applying individual formatting settings to a selection, you can simply apply the style. Many word processors, presentation graphics programs, and spreadsheets offer predefined styles, or let you create your own styles.

stylus A pen-like device used to write on a computer screen that accepts pen input. The stylus has an end like a ball-point pen. You might also use a stylus with a digitizing tablet, an input device that you can use with a drawing program to draw graphics.

159

subdirectory (see subfolder)

subfolder A subfolder is any folder within another folder. Each subfolder is one level below the main folder, and appears indented in the tree (Figure S.5). You can create subfolders within subfolders.

 To create a new folder or subfolder, open the disk or folder you want to hold the new folder. Click File | New, and click Folder. Type a folder name for the folder that appears and press [Enter].

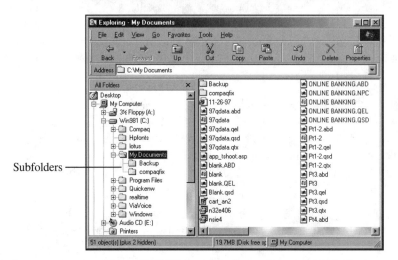

Figure S.5 Windows Explorer shows which folders hold other folders, called subfolders.

submenu Some menu commands display a triangle (arrowhead) to the right of the command name. If you point the mouse pointer to such a command, a smaller menu, called a submenu, appears. You can then click a command in the submenu to select a command.

subscribe If you want to read the information in a newsgroup, you must subscribe to the newsgroup, just as you would subscribe to a newspaper. First, download the list of newsgroups from a news server. Then, select the newsgroups to which you want to subscribe. Once you've subscribed, you can download and read the newsgroup's messages. (See also *unsubscribe*.)

subscript Smaller-sized characters that appear dropped below the normally formatted text. This example illustrates normal and subscript text: Normal$_{subscript}$.

160

suite A software suite consists of a group of programs that, together, offer a full range of capabilities at a favorable price. At a minimum, a business software suite includes a word processor and spreadsheet. It also typically includes information management or scheduling software. Other types of suites offer applications for using the Internet or graphics applications. (See also *Office* and *SmartSuite*.)

superscript Smaller-sized characters that appear aligned above the normally formatted text. This example illustrates normal and superscript text: Normal^{superscript}.

support Support, or technical support, means help that you can get from the software publisher of a program that you've purchased or the hardware manufacturer of a piece of hardware that you've purchased. Usually, you can dial a toll-free number for a limited time after your purchase to get free help. Beyond the applicable timeframe, you can purchase additional telephone help by credit card. Most software and hardware manufacturers also offer a Web site that you can consult for technical support information.

surf To use Web browser software to move from page to page on the World Wide Web.

surge protector (also called surge suppresser) A power surge, a sudden increase of power in the power lines, can damage your computer and other pieces of hardware. To protect the devices, you can plug them into a surge protector. The surge protector stops the power surge from traveling into your system. (See also *power surge*.)

> Multi-plug strips don't always provide surge suppression; make sure you buy one that does.

SVGA SVGA identifies a Super VGA display adapter (SVGA video capabilities for a system). An SVGA display can display at up to 1,024x768 resolution and up to 16.7 million colors. (See also *VGA* and *XGA*.)

swap file The swap file works along with the RAM to store program instructions and other information the RAM needs. (See also *virtual memory*.)

switch You include a switch at the end of a DOS command to provide more detail about how the command should operate. For example, if you type DIR /w at a DOS prompt and then press Enter, DOS lists the files in the current folder using the wide format, with multiple columns across the screen.

161

syntax Every type of command you use, formula you create, or query you develop follows rules called syntax. You must follow the correct syntax for the command, formula, or query to work correctly.

SyQuest drive SyQuest is a brand of removable disk drive. SyQuest currently offers a few different drive models: the 230M EZFlyer, the 1.5G SyJet, and the 1G SparQ. Over time, SyQuest has offered drives using cartridges in a number of sizes; the 44M and 88M drives were very popular with Mac users.

sysop A System Operator (sysop) runs a BBS, or a forum, on an online service. The sysop might respond to questions from users or direct a user to appropriate resources. Online chat events also have a type of sysop called a moderator, who makes sure that chatters don't harass each other or the chat guest. A sysop can ban a user from a forum or a chat.

system Another name for a PC. (See also *PC*.)

system software System software is another name for the operating system software that runs a personal computer or network computer.

system requirements Every application has system requirements that spell out the features a PC needs to run the software efficiently. For example, the system requirements define what type of processor the system needs, how much RAM and hard disk space the program consumes, and any devices, like a modem or a sound card, that the software needs to perform its functions.

system tray The system tray appears at the right end of the taskbar in Windows (Figure S.6). It displays the time and the volume control icon. It also may display icons for other items, like the power management features for a notebook. You can often right-click or double-click an icon in the system tray to work with the feature that it represents. For example, you can double-click the time to see a dialog box for resetting the system date and time.

Figure S.6 The system tray on the Windows taskbar shows the time and contains icons for other features.

system unit The system unit is the case or box holding the motherboard, CPU, power supply, internal disk drives, and other internal devices of a PC.

SYSTEM.INI The SYSTEM.INI file is one of the files that holds the settings that Windows uses to operate. Windows 95 and 98 rely on SYSTEM.INI less than Windows 3.1 did, but the PC does read SYSTEM.INI to find certain settings when it boots.

T

T1, T3 T1 and T3 lines (also noted as T-1 and T-3) are high-speed digital connections to the Internet. A large entity like a corporate network or university campus uses one of these types of lines to connect a network of many users to the Internet, which allows multiple users to access the Internet simultaneously. A T1 line can carry 1.55 Mbps and can handle 24 users. A T3 line carries 45Mbps, about 30 times as much as a T1 line.

tab In the leading spreadsheet programs today, every file actually holds more than one spreadsheet, or worksheet. This structure lets each file hold more information and makes it easier to navigate. A tab like a manila folder tab identifies each separate spreadsheet in a file. To select a spreadsheet, click its tab.

Tab key In many applications, you can press [Tab] to navigate. For example, you press [Tab] to move to the next cell in a spreadsheet or field in a database. In a word processor program, you press [Tab] to align text to the next tab stop. You can also press [Tab] to move between the different options in a dialog box.

tab stop A tab stop in a word-processing document is a location (or measurement) that you use to align text. For example, if you set a tab stop at one inch, you can press the [Tab] to align text at that one inch tab stop.

tab-delimited This is a plain-text (ASCII) file that can be exported from or imported to a database or spreadsheet. This type of file holds each record on a single line. Tab spaces separate the fields in each record. (See also *ASCII, comma-delimited, database, field,* and *record.*)

table In an application, a table organizes information into cells formed by rows and columns that are divided by gridlines, much like a spreadsheet. You can insert tables into documents in many spreadsheet programs and onto slides or pages in many presentation graphics programs. Most databases use a table format in which you can enter data. In addition, Web pages can display data in a table format. In particular, catalog Web sites often display information in a table format. For example, if you search a Web-based catalog for a type of product, it may display items and prices in a table.

tag When using HTML and XML to create Web pages, you insert codes called tags to specify how particular information should display. For example, you use the </HEAD> tag to identify the page header and the <center> tag to center text. Web browsers read the tags to know how to display the Web page information. (See also *HTML* and *XML*.)

tape backup drive You can connect a tape backup drive to a PC to back up information to cartridges holding magnetic tape. Tape works as a backup media, but isn't as effective as a regular storage media, because tape drives run more slowly and have to access data in the sequence in which it was recorded. In contrast, other disk drives can access information from any location on the disk.

target A target is a location to which you paste information previously copied or in which you insert an embedded OLE object. On a Web page, a target is a specific linked location. For example, if a page contains an alphabetical listing of information, you can click a letter at the top of the page to jump to the target link for that letter (the first item using that letter). (See also *OLE*.)

task A task is an application or operation on a computer. A task also might mean a command or process that you complete within an application to alter a file.

task switching Every application opened in Windows is a separate Windows task. You can use the taskbar to switch between the open applications, or press [Alt]+[Tab].

taskbar The taskbar is a bar with buttons and other features that appears below the desktop by default in Windows 95 and 98 (Figure T.1). Each application that you launch in Windows appears as a button on the taskbar. To switch to another open application, click its button on the taskbar. (See also *Start menu*.)

Start button

Figure T.1 The taskbar appears at the bottom of the desktop by default, and offers buttons for starting programs.

TCP/IP TCP/IP, or Transfer Control Protocol/Internet Protocol, is the underlying networking protocol for the Internet.

tear-off menu In some applications, you can drag a menu to a floating window. Such a menu is called a tear-off menu because you can "tear it off" from its default location and move it to the location you prefer.

technology Technology refers to new developments and improvements that accomplish tasks more quickly or achieve things not previously possible. Computing evolves rapidly, with new technologies developing monthly, if not daily.

telecommunications This term refers to using the telephone system to communicate. Telecommunication includes both voice and computer communications.

telephony Telephony describes the process of creating and using phone technology, as well as capabilities for using phone lines built into or added to a PC.

template You choose a template to make it the basis for a new file in an application. The template provides design elements, such as styles, page layout settings, and graphics. Some templates also provide basic information to help you create a finished document by "filling in the blanks." For example, templates in Excel and Lotus 1-2-3 contain formulas. When you enter a value in Excel and Lotus 1-2-3, the formulas in the templates calculate the answers.

terabyte A terabyte equals 1,000G or 1,099,511,627,776 bytes.

terminal emulation A mode of operation that a computer may use when communicating via modem. When using terminal emulation, information that you type goes directly to the modem for transmission.

text The characters that you type into most types of files. In a spreadsheet program, text refers to alphanumeric entries.

text box A text box is a type of option in a dialog box, as in Figure T.2. The text box prompts you to enter information for a command to use.

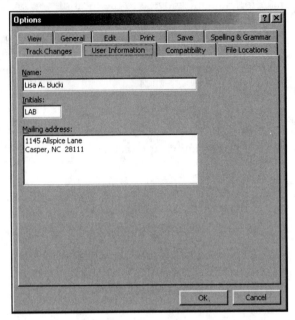

Figure T.2 Type information in a text box, like the three shown in this dialog box.

text file A text file contains characters but no formatting. You can use the Windows Notepad applet to create text files, which use a .TXT file name extension. Choose Start|Programs|Accessories|Notepad to start Notepad. Most applications can import plain text files. (See also *ASCII*.)

thermal wax printer This kind of printer uses an older color printing technology. A thermal wax printer uses heated print heads or styluses to transfer information to a specially coated paper with a waxy feel.

thesaurus Leading word processors offer a thesaurus feature so that you can find a better substitute for a selected word. You may also find a stand-alone thesaurus program that you can use at any time.

 If you don't have a stand-alone thesaurus capability but have a leading word processor, start your word processor, type in the word to look up, select the word, then choose the command for the thesaurus feature.

168

thread A newsgroup thread is a series of responses posted by users in response to an original posting. When you follow the thread (read each of the messages), you review the online conversation that transpired regarding the topic.

three-dimensional spreadsheet A three-dimensional spreadsheet program includes multiple spreadsheets or worksheets in each file. Three-dimensional spreadsheets enable you to select a 3D range (a range that spans multiple worksheets) and enter a 3D formula (a formula that calculates information from a 3D range). Three-dimensional spreadsheets not only enable you to include more information in each file but also make it easier to organize and summarize information. Excel and Lotus 1-2-3 are both three-dimensional spreadsheets. (See also *tab*.)

tick mark A tick mark crosses an axis on a chart to indicate a value increment. For example, a chart might use a tick mark to indicate 100, 200, and 300 on an axis. You can compare the markers on the chart to the tick marks to gauge the approximate value of each marker.

.TIFF This file name extension, as well as the .TIF extension, identifies a graphic file in the Tagged Image File Format. .TIFF files are bitmap files. Scanners produce files using the .TIFF format, among others, because it handles color and shading gradations well.

tile To display open windows so that they do not overlap, but instead collectively fill the available working area. For example, if you tile four windows, each window fills a quarter of the screen. In an application, choose Window|Tile to tile windows. To tile open application windows, right-click the taskbar and choose Tile Windows Horizontally or Tile Windows Vertically.

title bar Every window and dialog box has a title bar. The title bar displays the application name, file name, or dialog box name. If the window isn't maximized, you can drag the window title bar to move the window to a new location.

toggle Some commands and dialog box options, such as check boxes, function as toggles, meaning they can be either on (selected) or off (not selected). When you toggle on a menu command, a check mark appears to the left of the command name. For example, in some word processors and presentation graphics programs, you can choose View|Ruler to toggle the display of a ruler on and off.

169

token ring network A token ring network uses slightly more complicated technology than an Ethernet network. It connects the computers in a ring configuration; that is, each computer connects to the cabling ring, which carries the data. A token on the network carries a packet of data. To send information on the network, a PC must grab the token and attach data. After the data reaches its destination, the token detaches so that it can pick up and carry another packet. (See also *Ethernet* and *LAN*.)

toner The black or colored powder that a laser printer, plain paper fax machine, or photocopier uses to create images on paper. (See also *laser printer*.)

toner cartridge A plastic container that holds and dispenses the toner into a laser printer or other device. Once the cartridge runs out of toner, you remove it and insert another full one.

toolbar A toolbar is a strip of buttons appearing in an application window (Figure T.3). You click a toolbar button to perform a command, apply formatting, or accomplish some other operation. Toolbars usually appear at the top of the application window under the menu bar, but they may also appear at the side or the bottom of the window. You can often drag any toolbar to another on-screen location.

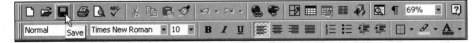

Figure T.3 Click a button on a toolbar to perform a command.

toolbox A toolbox resembles a toolbar, but holds items such as drawing tools rather than buttons that perform commands. For example, you might click the oval tool in a toolbox and then click and drag to draw an oval. Programming software that includes pre-written routines and objects to create applications might also be called a toolbar or toolkit.

tools The particular buttons or items offered in a toolbox.

touchpad A touchpad is a type of pointing device found on notebook computers. Drag your finger on the touchpad to move the mouse pointer. In some cases, you can tap the touchpad to click, double-click, or right-click. (See also *pointing device*.)

 If you prefer a touchpad to a mouse, you can add a touchpad to your desktop system. Conversely, if you don't like using your notebook's touchpad, you can use a mouse instead.

Computer & Internet Dictionary

tower This is a PC system unit case style. A tower case stands upright, on end, to minimize the amount of desktop or floor space it requires. (See also *desktop computer, minitower,* and *system unit.*)

track When you format a disk with your system, the formatting operation divides the magnetic information into concentric circles called tracks. This organization enables the computer to track where it stores information. (See also *cluster* and *sector.*)

track changes (see revision marks)

trackball A trackball looks and works (Figure T.4) something like an upside-down mouse. Rather than moving the trackball around on your desk, you move the ball in the center of the trackball to control the mouse pointer. (See also *input device* and *mouse.*)

Figure T.4 You can connect a trackball instead of a mouse to your system.

tractor feed Many dot-matrix printers use a tractor feed system to pull paper through. Tractor feed paper (also called continuous form paper because the sheets are connected and perforated) has a row of holes along each edge. Small sprockets on the printer poke through the holes in the paper. The sprockets turn to pull the paper along as the printer prints. You might see dot-matrix and tractor feed printers used for printing labels, paychecks, or any other type of repeating form. (See also *dot-matrix printer.*)

transparent When you apply a transparent fill, or background, to an object, you can see through the object. Transparent fills help you build more complicated graphic objects and effects, especially in draw and paint programs. (See also *opaque.*)

trash The Windows Recycle Bin maybe called the trash. The Macintosh operating system calls its version of the Recycle Bin the Trash. You can also use trash to describe the action of deleting a file, as in "I trashed that file yesterday, so I can't copy it for you now." (See also *Recycle Bin.*)

171

triple-click Move the mouse pointer over an on-screen object, and press and release the left mouse button three times in sequence. You rarely need to triple-click, but in some applications you can triple-click to select large amounts of information. (See also *click, double-click,* and *right-click.*)

Trojan Horse A Trojan Horse resembles a virus. It is a file or program that appears useful or informative but carries hidden instructions or a hidden program that damages the system. Trojan Horses can't copy themselves, but viruses can.

True Color Video cards and monitors with True Color, or 24-bit color, can display up to 16.7 million colors at a time. (See also *High Color.*)

TrueType font TrueType fonts offers two major benefits: both the computer screen and printer can use the TrueType font, eliminating the need for separately installed fonts and ensuring that the on-screen display exactly matches the printed result; secondly, TrueType fonts are scalable so you can change the size of the text. With older font technology, you had to install a separate font for each text size. (See also *printer font* and *screen font.*)

TSR A Terminate-and-Stay-Resident program loads when you start your system and remains in the background to perform its function as needed. For example, a virus scanning program may load automatically and later pop up to scan a file that you download or copy.

tutorial A tutorial leads you through the process of using software. For instance, you may buy a book that leads you step-by-step through building an example document. Some applications also come with on-screen tutorial help that will show you how to perform a particular operation or prompt you through each step.

TWAIN TWAIN software enables you to scan an image directly into an application that's not necessarily a graphics application. For example, if you have a scanner and TWAIN software installed, you can use the Insert|Picture|From Scanner command in Microsoft Word to insert a scanned image into the current document. (See also *scanner.*)

twisted pair In twisted pair cabling, two insulated copper wires wrap around one another, minimizing interference from other wires. Phone lines are twisted pair cabling. Normal phone line twisted pair wiring is unshielded, but you can get a shielded (better insulated) version to use for LAN connections. Twisted pair is easier to work with, though it carries less information than coaxial cabling. (See also *coaxial cable* and *LAN.*)

.TXT (see text file)

typeface A typeface is more specific than a font. A typeface is a complete set of characters using a particular font, style (bold or italic), and size. The distinction between fonts and typefaces was more important under older printing and typesetting technology, where the printer had to purchase a specific set of lead type letters or letter film for each typeface. Computers, in contrast, let you size and manipulate fonts.

U

UART The Universal Asynchronous Receiver Transmitter is a chip that helps a PC's serial port transmit information. The UART converts multiple streams of information coming from the system into a single asynchronous data stream that a modem can transmit. (See also *serial port*.)

UMB A system uses a memory management program, such as *EMM386.EXE*, to define an area in the UMA (upper memory area) as a UMB (upper memory block). You can use a command in *CONFIG.SYS* to load a system file into the UMB; this is called loading high. This technique makes more conventional memory area available to programs and other system files. (See also *conventional memory, expanded memory, extended memory, and upper memory*.)

undelete When you undelete a selected object in an application or a file, the application or Windows restores the text or file to its prior location.

> To undelete a selected object, choose Edit | Undo. To undelete a file, double-click the Recycle Bin icon on the Windows desktop. Click the file icon to undelete, then choose File | Restore.

underline You can underline selected text or numbers in an application. Many applications offer an underline button on a toolbar; click the button to apply or remove underlining.

underscore A keyboard character that appears to the right of the 0 key on the keyboard. (It's the hyphen's shifted character.) You can use underscore characters to create a line in a document. However, the underscore will not underline text.

undo This feature allows you to reverse a previous action. In some applications you can undo only the most recent action. In such a case, click an Undo button on a toolbar or choose the Edit | Undo command. In other applications you can undo multiple prior actions. In this case, you can click the Undo button multiple times or click the drop-down list arrow beside the undo button and use the list that appears to specify the number of actions to undo.

175

undocumented Any feature or use for a program that isn't included in the program's documentation book(s), online help, or Web site help. For example, Easter eggs are always undocumented, as are certain program shortcuts. In particular, graphics programs often offer many undocumented techniques. (See also *Easter egg*.)

unerase Unerase, or undelete, means recovering a file you previously deleted. The Norton Utilities includes a utility called Unerase for undeleting files. (See also *Norton Utilities* and *undelete*.)

UNIX UNIX is a command-line based operating system, but it can include a GUI, called a shell, to make it easier to use. UNIX works on a variety of systems, from mainframes to individual systems. Many organizations use a UNIX-based network. Some of the earliest systems connected to the Internet were UNIX-based, and UNIX (and its cousin linux) continue to play an important role in the world of connected computing. (See also *LINUX*.)

unsubscribe If you no longer want to subscribe to a newsgroup, you can discontinue the subscription (unsubscribe from the newsgroup) in your newsreader software (Figure U.1). Unsubscribing prevents unwanted messages from downloading to your computer, which saves time and cuts down on the amount of information stored in your newsreader. (See also *subscribe*.)

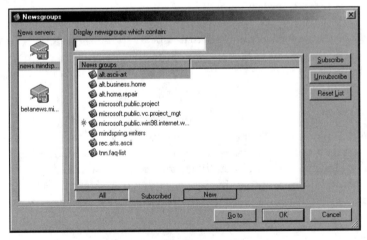

Figure U.1 You subscribe and unsubscribe to control which newsgroup messages to view.

unzip (see extract)

up arrow Pressing the ↑ on the keyboard moves the insertion point in a word processor document or presentation graphics page up one line, or moves the cell selector in a spreadsheet program up one row.

Pressing Ctrl + ↑ moves the insertion point to the beginning of the current paragraph, or from there to the beginning of the previous paragraph.

upgrade When you upgrade, you install a newer, and presumably better and faster, version of a software program or computer component. An upgrade may also consist of new or additional components for a system. For example, to upgrade a system's RAM, you add in more RAM rather than replacing all the existing RAM.

When you buy new software, avoid buying the cheaper upgrade version unless you're sure that you have a previous version of the program (or an eligible substitute from another software publisher). An upgrade version won't install correctly unless you're legitimately upgrading from a prior program version.

upload To transfer a file from your computer to another computer, usually to an online service or the Internet. For example, a message you post to a newsgroup might include a file attachment. When you post the message, the attached file uploads to the news server. (See also *Internet, news server,* and *virus*.)

uppercase Information presented in all CAPITAL LETTERS. Press Caps Lock to type in uppercase.

Upper Memory Area (UMA) The UMA consists of the memory between 640K and 1M within the first 1M of memory in the computer. (See also *UMB*.)

UPS A UPS (uninterruptible power supply) is approximately the opposite of a surge suppressor. The UPS protects your system in the event of a power outage, which would cause you to lose any unsaved information.
A UPS has a battery that charges while you're using the computer. When the power goes out, the battery power gives you enough time to save your work and shut down the system properly. (See also *surge protector*.)

A basic UPS starts at about $90, but if you plan to add computers or a network, you might consider buying a more expensive UPS that can protect multiple systems and network components.

177

USB (universal serial bus) This new type of connection can connect dozens of devices to your computer in a daisy-chain (plug the first device into the port, connect the next device to the first one, and so on). In other instances, you can plug in a hub that offers numerous USB connections. USB ports can transfer data at rates up to 12 Mbps (12 million bits per second). Up to 127 peripheral devices (mice, modems, keyboards, digital cameras) can connect to a single USB port. USB ports recognize Plug-and-Play devices. After installing the software that runs a USB device (the drivers), you can plug in and unplug the device as needed without having to reinstall the software or restart the system (called hot plugging). Windows 98 provides full USB support. (See also *bps* and *FireWire*.)

USENET The USEr NETwork (USENET) is a world-wide network of news server computers that manage newsgroup postings. USENET servers exchange newsgroup listings and postings within newsgroups, allowing you to access current newsgroup information. Many ISPs offer USENET news servers. Other USENET servers aren't connected to the Internet, such as servers for private corporate discussion groups. (See also *newsgroup*.)

user group A user group meets regularly to discuss a particular type of hardware or software and exchange relevant information.

user ID The name or number that you use to log on to a network, online service, or the Internet. You also might use a user name (your user ID, e-mail address, or a name you create) to log on to a specific type of server, like a news server or FTP server, or to log on to a Web site that requires registration.

user interface The on-screen information that a computer system displays, enabling you to give commands, see the results from commands, and enter information. (See also *graphical user interface* and *Windows*.)

user profile Descriptive information about yourself that you enter when you log on to online services, some Web sites, and chat rooms. Other users or the service administrator can look at the information to get an idea of who you are. Web sites and online services might use profile information to market services and products to you.

 If confidentiality is important to you, omit some user profile information. For example, you can give a handle rather than your real name, and leave out information, like your address or e-mail address, to prevent unwanted contact.

user-friendly User-friendly programs and equipment are designed to be easy to use without extensive training. A user-friendly program makes key tasks obvious, such as clicking a big Exit button to exit the program.

utility A program (or operating system feature) designed to maintain the system, diagnose and fix problems, perform routine operations, or perform specific, limited tasks. For example, the ScanDisk feature in Windows is a utility that repairs disks. Virus checking software is a utility that performs a specific function. (See also *ScanDisk* and *virus*.)

> To find the utility features installed in Windows, choose Start | Programs | Accessories | System Tools.

.UUE The file name extension for a file encoded using the UUencode (UU) encoding format. (See also *decode*, *encode*, and *WinCode*.)

URL (pronounced earl) The acronym for Uniform Resource Locator, the address for a Web page (or other resource) on the Internet. The URL consists of several parts. The first is the content identifier: http:// or https:// for Web sites, or ftp:// for an FTP site, for example. The second part is the Web site, as in www.ddcpub.com. The final part is the location, or the path to a particular page, as in /html/order.html. A full address might look like *http://www.ddcpub.com/html/order.html*. (See also *FTP*, *http://*, and *Web site*.)

> A Web site name may begin with something other than www. The site name may end with .com (company), .org (non-profit organization), .net (service provider), .edu (educational institution) or other extension to identify the type of organization running the site. Also, current Web browser versions let you skip typing the content identifier when you enter the URL; you can type *www.ddcpub.com* and press Enter, for example, to display DDC's home page.

V

V. protocols The V. standards are communications standards (usually modem communications) that specify how quickly data can travel and what special data handling features can be used. Some of the more recent V. standards include:

- V.32bis Enables two-way transmissions at 14,400 bps.
- V.32fast Enables two-way transmissions at 28,800 bps.
- V.34 Enables two-way transmissions at 33,600 bps.
- V.42 Specifies a type of error correction that retransmits data corrupted by noise in the phone lines.
- V.42bis Enables a modem to compress data, so that it can transfer more information.
- V.90 The new standard for 56K modem transmission.
- V.120 A standard for ISDN modems.

(See also *CCITT*.)

VAR This acronym stands for value added reseller. It refers to a consulting firm, retailer, or other reseller that will create and install customized PCs and networks for clients, as well as providing custom documentation and technical support. (See also *OEM*.)

variable A storage area for a value or string used by the program. Once the programmer creates and names the variable, the program can use or change the variable contents.

VBA (see Visual Basic for Applications)

.VBX This file name extension identifies a custom control used in Visual Basic programming. *.VBX* controls are older than *.OCX* controls, which work with OLE; newer programs use *.OCX* controls. A programmer can insert a *.VBX* control in a programming project, and set properties to define how the control works. Then, the programmer distributes the original *.VBX* file along with the finished program's *.EXE* file and other program files. (See also *.OCX*.)

181

vector graphic A vector graphic consists of layered, resizable objects. Unlike in a bitmap graphic, the objects in a vector graphic image remain independent, so you can format, move, or resize the object. Vector graphics are not only easier to edit but also tend to have smaller file sizes than bitmap graphics. (See also *bitmap graphic* and *draw program*.)

version A named or numbered edition of a product. Most older software used version numbers to represent different versions, with a full number increase representing a substantial product update and a decimal increase representing a minor update. Now, many software vendors use the year to distinguish different software versions, as in Windows 95 and Windows 98. (See also *upgrade*.)

VESA (see local bus)

VGA VGA identifies a Video Graphics Array display adapter (VGA video capabilities for a system). A VGA can display at 640x480 resolution and 256 colors. (See also *SVGA* and *XGA*.)

video This general term relates to displaying still and full-motion information on the screen. A PC's video capabilities determine how well it can display images and play video clips. Video software enables you to edit video clips.

video adapter The video adapter, or adapter card, controls what color depth and resolution the monitor can display, and how well the system can display motion video. The video adapter capabilities must match the capabilities of the monitor. (See also *monitor*.)

video memory (see memory)

video mode A particular combination of colors and resolution that you display on your monitor, such as 640x480 resolution and 256 colors.

 To change the video mode, right-click the desktop, and click Properties. Click the Settings tab, then change the Color Palette and Desktop Area settings (Windows 95) or Colors and Screen Area settings (Windows 98). Click OK.

VRAM (see memory)

virtual disk A virtual disk is the opposite of virtual memory, when a system uses part of RAM as if it were a disk drive. A virtual disk may also be called a RAM disk. You have to use memory management software to create a virtual disk. Then, you can copy files to and from the virtual disk. The virtual disk works much more quickly than a real disk drive, but it loses all its contents whenever you shut down your system. (See also *virtual memory*.)

virtual machine A virtual machine exists in RAM. Software can set aside part of the system's RAM so that it acts as a separate computer, running software separately. Windows, to some degree, creates a virtual machine to run multiple programs. (See also *Java Virtual Machine*.)

virtual memory Windows creates virtual memory to expand a PC's memory capabilities. It uses space on the hard disk as extra memory. (See also *swap file*.)

virtual reality A simulated 3D world created either in a game or on a Web site. You can manipulate objects and interact with the virtual world.

virus A computer program that infects other files and programs. Viruses usually spread when you download files and programs or share files on disk. The virus can destroy files on your system to the point of deleting information or preventing the system from booting. Virus checking and scanning software can find and eliminate viruses.

Some newer types of viruses called macro viruses can infect files and templates in Word and Excel. Both Word and Excel offer a feature that will alert you if a file that you're opening includes macros and therefore, potentially, macro viruses.

Visual Basic This high-level programming language from Microsoft speeds the process of creating Windows applications. The programmer can draw screens and dialog boxes on the screen, adding programmable buttons and other controls. The programmer can use BASIC-like language to write the procedure that should occur when a user selects each control. (See also *.OCX, programming language*, and *.VBX*.)

Visual Basic for Applications Microsoft includes this subset of Visual Basic, also called VBA, with applications like Word, Excel, Access, and Project. The user can use the VBA commands to enhance recorded macros or write more complicated macros and applets. (See also *macro*.)

VLB This acronym stands for VESA Local Bus, a type of video adapter that connects more directly with the CPU for faster display. (See also *local bus*.)

voice-capable modem A voice-capable modem can carry voice information instead of or in addition to data. You can use a voice-capable modem, with the right software, as both a modem and a speaker phone, speaking into your system's microphone or a headset mic. (See also *DSVD*.)

183

The software used with a voice-capable modem can also take messages and receive faxes. If you have a home business and are in the market for a new system, look for one with a voice-capable modem and messaging software.

voice recognition Software technology that enables a computer equipped with a sound card to recognize words and commands that you speak into a microphone. Some voice recognition programs only allow you to enter information in a file. Others also work in conjunction with other applications on your system, so that you can give software a command by speaking the command. IBM ViaVoice and Dragon Naturally Speaking are examples of voice recognition software.

volume The loudness of sound played or recorded by your system. Volume is also another name for a disk. (See also *volume label*.)

volume control The windows system tray includes an icon that will display volume controls (Figure V.1) for turning certain sound features on your system up or down. For example, you can drag the Stereo Output slider to increase the volume at which the system plays your audio CDs. (See also *system tray*.)

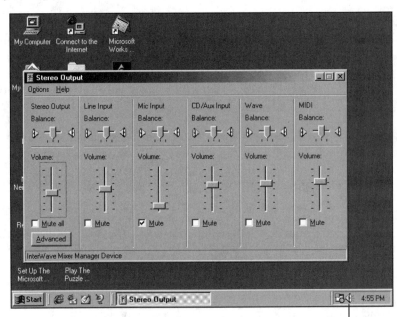

Figure V.1 Turn up the sound in the Stereo Output dialog box.

volume label A volume label is a name assigned to a disk. Windows displays the disk's volume label in the My Computer or Windows Explorer window, so you can tell at a glance what files a floppy or removable disk holds. To apply a volume label to a disk, insert it into the drive if it's a floppy or removable disk. Double-click the My Computer icon on the desktop. Right-click the icon for the disk to label in the My Computer window, then click Properties in the shortcut menu. Type the name to use in the Label text box of the General tab of the properties dialog box, then click OK.

VRML This acronym stands for Virtual Reality Modeling Language. Web designers can use this language to create VRML worlds online. To display a VRML world, your browser must have a VRML add-on or plug-in. There are a number of VRML add-ons that you can download from the Web. (See also *plug-in*.)

W

wallpaper A graphic image can be displayed as wallpaper on a Windows desktop to personalize and decorate the desktop. You can use .*BMP*, .*GIF*, and .*HTML* files as backgrounds in Windows 98. Right-click the desktop and click Properties. Click a wallpaper listed in the Wallpaper area of the Background tab, or use the Browse button to find the file you want. Click OK to display the wallpaper.

WAN A Wide Area Network (WAN) spans more than one physical location. For example, a WAN might connect a company's New York and San Francisco offices. (See also *LAN*.)

warm boot When you warm boot the system, you restart it without powering it down. A warm boot empties the memory and restarts the operating system. Press [Ctrl]+[Alt]+[Delete] twice to warm boot the system in Windows. (See also *boot, cold boot,* and *restart*.)

.WAV This file name extension identifies a type of sound file that Windows can play if the PC has a sound card. You can use the Windows Sound Recorder applet to record your own .WAV files. (See also *Sound Recorder*.)

Web (see World Wide Web)

Web search To find information on a particular topic on the World Wide Web, you can perform a Web search to find links to applicable pages. (See also *search engine*.)

Web site A Web site is a collection of Web pages published by an individual, company, or other organization. The home page or start page for the site contains links to the other pages.

webcast A webcast, also called a simulcast or multicast, occurs when an information provider broadcasts sound and video information over the Web, often concurrently with a live event. For example, a site might broadcast a live interview with celebrities while users use chat capabilities on the site to send in questions.

Webmaster The Webmaster is the individual (or group) responsible for maintaining a Web site.

> Often, you can send an e-mail message to a site's Webmaster using an address in the format *webmaster@website.com*.

whiteboard You can use conferencing software (like NetMeeting in Windows 98) to hold conferences over the Internet. Many conferencing programs include a whiteboard feature. The whiteboard displays information, such as a file or message, simultaneously to all conference participants.

widow A page break that occurs at an inopportune location, bumping the last line of a paragraph to the top of the next page or column. You can either insert a hard page break or column break before the beginning of the full paragraph or increase the page margin until the widow fits. (See also *hard page break* and *orphan*.)

wildcard A wildcard character can represent unknown characters when you perform a file find or Web search. (See also *** and *?*.)

WinCode You can use the WinCode utility to encode and decode files sent or received via the Internet. Because WinCode is Windows-based, it's easier to use than other encoding programs. (See also *binHex*, *encode*, *decode*, and *.UUE*.)

> WinCode is available for downloading from multiple locations on the Web. Perform a Web search for "WinCode" to find a download location.

window All versions of the Windows operating system present applications, programs, and files in rectangular boxes called windows. Dividing information into windows allows you to switch between applications and files. Click any part of the window in which you want to work. (See also *Windows*, *Windows for Workgroups*, and *Windows NT*.)

window border A window's boundary is called a border (Figure W.1). You can use the window border to resize the window.

Computer & Internet Dictionary

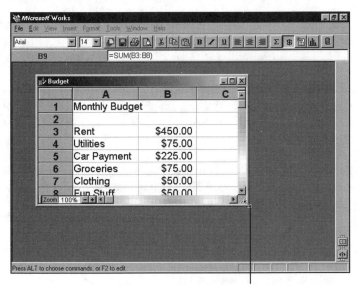

Drag the window border to resize the window.

Figure W.1 Application windows hold files and applications.

Windows Windows is a popular operating system software from Microsoft. Earlier versions of Windows served only as a GUI, but Windows 95 and 98 integrate DOS features more fully. Windows 98 offers better Internet and hardware support than Windows 95, as well as more utilities for monitoring and maintaining the system. (See also *GUI.*)

Windows Explorer Windows Explorer, a feature within Windows, is used to manage folders and files. Explorer displays a graphical folder tree to illustrate how disks, files, and folders relate. To start Windows Explorer, choose Start|Programs|Windows Explorer. (See also *subfolder* and *My Computer.*)

Windows for Workgroups This older variation of Windows provided networking features not included in the standard Windows version.

Windows NT The Windows NT software serves as both the Network Operating System (Windows NT Server) on a LAN server and as the operating system (NT Workstation) for individual PCs connected to a Windows NT network. Windows NT has become a popular alternative to other types of NOS software because it provides maintenance features and features facilitating Internet connections that are easy to use. (See also *LAN* and *Netware.*)

Windows Paint A Windows applet that provides basic tools for creating bitmap graphics. To start Paint, choose Start|Program|Accessories|Paint. (See also *bitmap graphic* and *.BMP*.)

Windows WordPad This Windows applet is a simple word processor that you can use to create plain text documents and documents with modest formatting. WordPad can open Microsoft Word files, too. Start by choosing Start|Program|Accessories|WordPad. (See also *Notepad*.)

WIN.INI The WIN.INI file holds the settings Windows uses to operate. Windows 95 and 98 rely on WIN.INI less than Windows 3.1 did, but the PC does read WIN.INI to find certain settings.

WinZip You can use the WinZip program (Figure W.2) to compress and extract files so that they take up less disk space or take less time to send over the Internet. (See also *compress* and *extract*.)

WinZip is shareware. Download it from *http://www.winzip.com*.

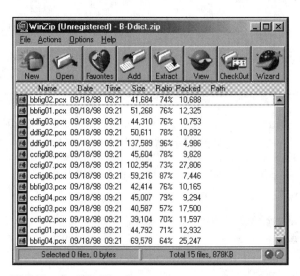

Figure W.2 Use the WinZip shareware to compress and extract files.

wireless Wireless devices share information without using wires. For example, if both your notebook and desktop PCs have infrared ports, you can send information between them without using a cable to connect them. You can buy wireless networking kits to create a wireless home or small business network. (See also *infrared port*.)

190

wizard A wizard helps you perform a particular operation, such as creating a new document or setting up an Internet connection. A wizard minimizes an operation into a series of easy choices. (See also *Internet Connection Wizard*.)

.WMF This file name extension identifies a graphics file in the Windows Metafile format, a type of vector graphic format. (See also *vector graphic*.)

Word The Microsoft Word word processor program (Figure W.3) anchors the Microsoft Office suite. Word offers a number of templates and wizards to help you create documents, perform a mail merge, or create a table in the document table. (See also *Office*.)

Figure W.3 Microsoft Word leads the word processor market.

Word Pro Word Pro joins 1-2-3, Freelance, Organizer, and other programs in the SmartSuite suite of software from Lotus Development Corp. Word Pro offers many of the same features as Word, but has traditionally surpassed Word in document design. For example, Word Pro was first to offer frames that you can use to insert and format graphics, text, and other information. (See also *SmartSuite*.)

word processor In a word-processing program, you can create documents such as memos, reports, and chapters. Word processors offer tools for entering, editing, organizing, and formatting text.

wordwrap The wordwrap feature automates the process of creating new lines in a word processor. When you enter enough text to fill the current line, the word processor starts a new line.

WordPerfect WordPerfect is the word-processing program that's part of the Corel WordPerfect Suite. WordPerfect offers many of the same capabilities as its counterparts, Word and Word Pro. It may be the best choice for users who have used previous versions of WordPerfect, or have many documents created using older versions of WordPerfect.

worksheet A worksheet is the same thing as a spreadsheet. Excel calls each spreadsheet in a file a worksheet, for example. (See also *spreadsheet* and *tab*.)

workstation A workstation is an individual computer (desktop or notebook) connected to a LAN. A workstation also may refer to an extremely powerful PC running software like CAD or UNIX. (See also *CAD, LAN,* and *UNIX.*)

World Wide Web (WWW) The World Wide Web is a network of Web server computers that store, organize, and deliver Web pages to users.

WORM This acronym for Write Once Read Many identifies any kind of storage media to which a drive can write information only once, such as a CD-R and optical disks. (See also *CD-R drive* and *optical disk.*)

write error Windows displays a write error message if you try to save or copy a file that a disk won't accept. For example, you'll see a write error message if you try to write to a disk that's damaged, full, or write-protected.

write-protect When you write-protect a disk (usually a 3 ½-inch floppy disk), you move a tab on the disk to prevent the drive from writing any new information to the disk. To write protect a 3 ½-inch disk, hold the disk with the label side facing away from you and the sliding door down, and slide the tab in the upper-left corner up.

WYSIWYG This acronym (pronounced *wissywig*) stands for "What You See Is What You Get." It applies to any display enhancements that ensure that the information displayed on the screen for a file exactly matches its printed output.

X

XGA XGA identifies a less common type of display adapter. An XGA display can display at up to 1,024x768 resolution and up to 256 colors. (See also *SVGA* and *VGA*.)

XML This acronym for eXtensible Markup Language enables Web page designers to create custom HTML tags. (See also *HTML* and *tag*.)

xmodem Xmodem is a transmission protocol for sending files directly over a modem using a communications program, like Windows HyperTerminal.

> When sending or receiving files via modem connection and a program such as HyperTerminal, both the sending and receiving systems must use the same transmission protocol.

XMS This standard helps a PC access extended memory using extended memory manager software, like *HIMEM.SYS*. (See also *extended memory*.)

X
Y
Z

193

Y

Y2K Y2K refers to the "Year 2000 Problem" or "the Millennium bug." Some older systems and software can't recognize dates past December 31, 1999. Systems suffering from the Y2K problem may not start on the first date of the year 2000, or may not be able to calculate information correctly. For example, a bank's computer system might not be able to calculate interest.

ymodem   Ymodem is a transmission protocol used to send files directly over a modem using a communications program like Windows HyperTerminal.

Z

ZIF socket A Zero Insertion Force (ZIF) socket is a motherboard socket into which you can plug in a 486 or Pentium CPU. A ZIF socket makes it easier to upgrade the system CPU. However, Pentium II processors require a different type of slot. (See also *Pentium II*.)

.ZIP This file name extension identifies a type of compressed file created with a utility like WinZip. (See also *compressed file* and *WinZip*.)

Zip drive A Zip drive (Figure Z.1) is a type of removable disk drive that you can add to a PC. Each Zip disk holds about 100M of information. Iomega, which makes the Zip, has sold more than 10 million drives, making the Zip format one of the more popular alternatives to a floppy disk. (See also *Jaz drive*.)

Figure Z.1 A Zip disk (used in a Zip drive) can hold 100M of information.

zmodem Zmodem is a transmission protocol used to send files directly over a modem using a communications program like Windows HyperTerminal.

zoom To change a document's size on the screen. Zoom in (or increase the zoom percentage) to make the document look larger. Zoom out (or decrease the zoom percentage) to make the document look smaller.

> Use the View menu in an application for a Zoom command to zoom in and out. Also, look on the toolbar for a button or drop-down list (it may display a percentage) to change the zoom.

zoomed video port Some notebook computers include a zoomed video port, a type of PC Card port that provides a faster connection for video devices such as video cameras. This port works by transferring data directly from the PC Card inserted in the slot to a special zoomed video bus.

195

Visual Reference

Did we make one for you?

CAT. NO.	TITLE
G29...	**Microsoft® Access 97**
G21...	**Microsoft Excel 97**
G33...	**The Internet**
G37...	**Internet Explorer 4.0**
G19...	**Microsoft Office 97**
G23...	**Microsoft Outlook 97**
G22...	**Microsoft PowerPoint 97**
G20...	**Microsoft Word 97**
G36...	**Microsoft Windows 98**

$15 ea.

To order call
800-528-3897
or fax 800-528-3862
VISIT US ON THE WEB:
http://www.ddcpub.com

DDC Publishing
275 Madison Avenue
New York, NY 10016

10/98 V

Internet in an Hour for Everyone!

Each book gives you the basics of Internet usage, then introduces you to a world of practical World Wide Web sites, searching tips, and advice on browsing—all relating to the book's particular audience and subject matter.

$10 ea

The Internet in an Hour Series

for Students HR1	Business Communication
for Managers. HR2	& E-mail HR6
for Beginners HR3	for Seniors HR7
for Sales People HR4	Entertainment & Leisure HR8
101 Things You Need to Know. . HR5	for Shoppers
	& Bargain Hunters HR9

To order call
800-528-3897
fax 800-528-3862
Visit our Web site:
www.ddcpub.com

275 Madison Ave.
New York, NY 10016

10/98 HR

Fast-teach Learning Books

How we designed each book

Our self-paced hands-on text gives you the concept and the objective in simple language. We show you how to format the exercise. Next to the exercise we provide the keystrokes and the illustrated layout; step by simple step - graded and cumulative.

If a word didn't tell, it got tossed out. We don't teach reading. You go into software functions immediately. No time wasted.

Did we make one for you? $27 ea

Title	Cat. No.	Title	Cat. No.
Creating a Web Page w/ Office 97	Z23	Lotus 1-2-3 Rel. 4 & 5 for Windows	B9
Corel Office 7	Z12	Microsoft Office 97	Z19
Corel WordPerfect 7	Z16	Microsoft Office for Windows 95	Z6
Corel WordPerfect 8	Z31	PowerPoint 97	Z22
DOS + Windows	Z7	Typing with Microsoft Word 97	Z24
Excel 97	Z21	Windows 3.1 – A Quick Study	WQS-1
Excel 5 for Windows	E9	Windows 95	Z3
Excel 7 for Windows 95	Z11	Windows 98	Z26
Internet	Z15	Word 97	Z20
Internet for Business	Z27	Word 6 for Windows	1-WDW6
Internet for Kids	Z25	Word 7 for Windows 95	Z10
Keyboarding/Word Processing for Kids	Z33	WordPerfect 6 for Windows	Z9
Lotus 1-2-3 Rel. 2.2–4.0 for DOS	L9	WordPerfect 6.1 for Windows	H9
		Works 4 for Windows 95	Z8

Learning the Internet
We teach you how to get information from the Internet. Includes CD-ROM Simulation.
$27
Cat. No. Z30

Learning Keyboarding & Word Processing Microsoft® Word 97
It does exactly what it tells you.
$27
Cat. No. Z24

Learning the Internet for Business
From email to online business resources, Web marketing to a list of essential downloads. This book covers it all.
$27
Cat. No. Z27

Learning the Internet for Kids
Kids sail the seven seas and learn how to search the Internet, send email, download and browse the Internet.
$27
Cat. No. Z25

275 Madison Avenue, New York, NY 10016

Phone: 800-528-3897
Fax 800-528-3862

Our One-Day Course has you using your software the next day

$18 ea.
Includes diskette

Here's how we do it

We struck out all the unnecessary words that don't teach anything. No introductory nonsense. We get right to the point-in "See spot run" language. No polysyllabic verbiage. We give you the keystrokes and the illustrated layout; step by simple step.

You learn faster because you read less

No fairy tales, novels, or literature. Small words, fewer words, short sentences, and fewer of them. We pen every word as if an idiot had to read it. You understand it faster because it reads easier.

Illustrated exercises show you how

We tell you, show you, and explain what you see. The layout shows you what we just explained. The answers fly off the page and into your brain as if written on invisible glass. No narration or exposition. No time wasted. **Each book comes with a practice disk to eliminate typing the exercises.**

DID WE MAKE ONE FOR YOU?

Cat. No.	Title
DC-2	Access 97, Day 1 ISBN 1-56243-519-1
DC-29	Access 97, Day 2 ISBN 1-56243-579-5
DC-30	Access 97, Day 3 ISBN 1-56243-580-9
DC-1	Access 7 for Windows 95 ISBN 1-56243-518-3
DC-23	Creating a Web Page w/Word 97
DC-4	Excel 97, Day 1 ISBN 1-56243-521-3
DC-27	Excel 97, Day 2 ISBN 1-56243-577-9
DC-28	Excel 97, Day 3 ISBN 1-56243-578-7
DC-3	Excel 7 for Windows 95 ISBN 1-56243-520-5
DC-22	FrontPage w/Sim. CD ISBN 1-56243-448-9
DC-5	Internet E-mail & FTP w/Sim. CD
DC-6	Intro to Computers and Windows 95 ISBN 1-56243-523-X
DC-21	Local Area Network ISBN 1-56243-502-7
DC-35	Lotus Notes 4.5 ISBN 1-56243-589-2
DC-7	Macintosh System 7.5 ISBN 1-56243-524-8
DC-8	MS Explorer w/ Sim. CD ISBN 1-56243-525-6
DC-9	MS Project 4 ISBN 1-56243-526-4
DC-10	Netscape Navigator w/ Sim. CD
DC-11	Outlook 97 ISBN 1-56243-528-0
DC-12	PageMaker 5 ISBN 1-56243-529-9
DC-14	PowerPoint 97, Day 1 ISBN 1-56243-531-0
DC-31	PowerPoint 97, Day 2 ISBN 1-56243-581-7
DC-13	PowerPoint 7 for Windows 95
DC-16	Windows 95 ISBN 1-56243-533-7
DC-24	Windows NT 4.0 ISBN 1-56243-297-4
DC-15	Windows NT 3.5 ISBN 1-56243-532-9
DC-18	Word 97, Day 1 ISBN 1-56243-535-3
DC-25	Word 97, Day 2 ISBN 1-56243-575-2
DC-26	Word 97, Day 3 ISBN 1-56243-576-0
DC-17	Word 7 for Windows 95 ISBN 1-56243-534-5
DC-19	WordPerfect 6.1 ISBN 1-56243-536-1
DC-34	Upgrading to Office 97 ISBN 1-56243-588-4
DC-20	Visual Basic 3.0 ISBN 1-56243-537-X

10/98 OD

DDC Quick Reference Guides find software answers faster because you read less

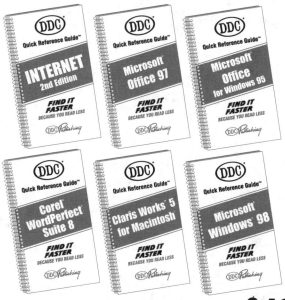

Find it quickly and get back to the keyboard—fast

The index becomes your quick locator. Just follow the step-by-step illustrated instructions. We tell you what to do in five or six words. Sometimes only two. No narration or exposition. Just "press this—type that" illustrated commands. The spiral binding keeps pages open so you can type what you read. You save countless hours of lost time by locating the illustrated answer in seconds.

The time you save when this guide goes to work for you will pay for it the very first day

$12 ea.

Did We Make One for You?

TITLE	CAT.No
Access 2 for Windows	OAX2
Access 7 for Windows 95	AX95
Access 97	G28
Claris Works 5 for Macintosh	G39
Computer Terms	D18
Corel WordPerfect Suite 8	G32
Corel WordPerfect 7 Win 95	G12
Corel WordPerfect Suite 7 for Win 95	G11
DOS 5	J17
DOS 6.0 - 6.22	ODS62
Excel 5 for Windows	F18
Excel 7 for Windows 95	XL7
Excel 97	G27
Internet, 2nd Edition	I217
Lotus 1-2-3 Rel. 3.1 DOS	J18
Lotus 1-2-3 Rel. 3.4 DOS	L287
Lotus 1-2-3 Rel. 4 DOS	G4
Lotus 1-2-3 Rel. 4 Win	O3013
Lotus 1-2-3 Rel. 5 Win	L19
Lotus 1-2-3 Rel. 6 Win 95	G13
Lotus Notes 4.5	G15
Lotus Smart Suite 97	G34

TITLE	CAT.No
Office for Win. 3.1	MO17
Office for Win 95	MO95
Office 97	G25
PageMaker 5 for Win & Mac	PM18
PowerPoint 4 for Win	OPPW4
PowerPoint 7 for Win 95	PPW7
PowerPoint 97	G31
Quattro Pro 6 for Win	QPW6
Quicken 4 for Windows	G7
Windows NT 4	G16
Windows 3.1 & 3.11	N317
Windows 95	G6
Windows 98	G35
Word 6 for Windows	OWDW6
Word 7 for Windows 95	WDW7
Word 97	G26
WordPerfect 5.1+ for DOS	W-5.1
WordPerfect 6 for DOS	W18
WordPerfect 6 for Win	OWPW6
WordPerfect 6.1 for Win	W19
Works 3 for DOS	M18
Works 3 for Win	OWKW3
Works 4 for Win 95	WKW4

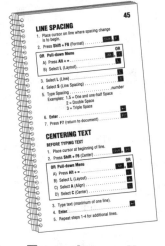

To order call
800-528-3897
or fax 800-528-3862
Visit our Web site:
http://www.ddcpub.com

DDC *Publishing*

275 Madison Ave., New York, NY 10016

10/98 Q

NEW at ddcpub.com!

Visit the DDC Web Rover Gallery
Go to www.ddcpub.com
and click on the *Web Rover Gallery* link

The **DDC Web Rover** hunts the Internet every week, sniffing out the best sites on the Web.

In the **DDC Web Rover Gallery**, you'll find links to great Web Rover recommended resources for students, bargain hunters, sales people, managers, seniors. You'll also find great entertainment, leisure, and vacation sites.

If you are on the scent of a Web site you find interesting, DDC would like to hear from you. Click on the Web Rover's link and submit the site and the reason you like it.

We search the Web
so you don't have to!